Ideas to Grow Your Mind

Mindsets to be more productive,
build better habits and learn deeply

Liam Finnian

GRAPEVINE INDIA

Published by

GRAPEVINE INDIA PUBLISHERS PVT LTD

www.grapevineindia.com
Delhi | Mumbai
email: grapevineindiapublishers@gmail.com

Ordering Information:
Quantity sales: Special discounts are available on quantity
purchases by corporations, associations, and others.
For details, reach out to the publisher.

First published by Grapevine India 2022
Copyright © Grapevine 2022
All rights reserved

Printed and bound in India by Nutech Print Services, New Delhi

INTRODUCTION

Section 1: Productivity

Section 2: Creativity

Section 3: Habits

Section 4: Learning

Section 5: Mental Models

Section 6: Mindset

Introduction

When I meet average people, I realize that their learning has stagnated. They start getting exposed to the same people and the same habits, and hence they have the same thoughts. Their lives are taken over by inertia and they are often just going with the flow. Most of their days are photocopies of each other.

On the other hand, when I meet smart people, I notice that there is something different about the way they look at the world. They have certain mindsets and mental models which make them who they are.

The same problem will have a completely different response from them, even if they have the same resources. The way the neurons in their mind would make connections would be different, as the frameworks stored in their mind are what makes them who they are. The ideas coinciding in their head will happen in a way that is much more likely to bring out solutions.

By the late 2000s, it was clear that we were entering the era of internet entrepreneurs. I had the good fortune of knowing and even mentoring some of them. I met some young kids who went on to become unicorn founders. I met some posterboys of the start-up ecosystem who crashed and burned VC money in meaningless ads.

In these interactions, I got to know a lot about what kind of traits successful people seem to have. Although I talk about entrepreneurs here, the rules and thoughts shared in this book are applicable to athletes, artists, actors, singers, students, corporate employees or anyone who wants to understand the world better.

I pondered over what caused the gap between successful entrepreneurs and strugglers, and what I could do to bridge it (for them and for myself). I interviewed more than a hundred people whose intellect I respected in order to get a deep peek into the way they look at the world. I made extensive notes and read dozens of books to further process what I had understood. I listened to podcasts, read articles, and watched videos on the subject.

I realized that if I distil this knowledge in the form of a book, it could help a lot of people grow their minds. And that's how this book came about.

After extensive research, I realised that just the knowledge of these twenty-nine mental models under six categories can drastically expand a person's worldview. I have repeatedly experimented with these in group workshops. I have done one-on-one coaching of hundreds of people. Each and every participant has returned to share a story of transformation. I know that growing someone's mind is a tall claim, but these mental models have genuinely made these people feel that their mind has 'grown.' That is what I am trying to do through this book.

I have narrowed down six areas where these changes would be most potent and tangible. There are multiple chapters under each section. Each chapter is an idea in itself. Each chapter can be a whole book, but I have tried to explain it in a way that will help you actually use it in your daily life.

The six sections are:
1. Productivity
2. Creativity
3. Mental Models
4. Learning
5. Habits
6. Mindset

This book will reshape the way you look at life and think about progress and success, and give you the tools and strategies you need to transform your life. Whether you are a team looking to be more innovative, an organization hoping to build better systems, or simply an individual who wants to upgrade their intellect, it will help you look deeper at the world and change the way you perceive things. As a result, you will make more informed decisions and develop mindsets to understand the world better.

I hope you come out smarter from this book.

Section 1-Productivity

Years are wasted because people don't waste hours.

Let's talk about Gina. She is a business owner who makes and sells birdhouses. To make a birdhouse, Gina needs input such as wood, paint, nails, tools, and her own labour. An input is any resource used to create goods and services.

It took Gina an hour to make each birdhouse. The completed birdhouses are her output. Output is the quantity of goods or services produced.

With experience, Gina discovered better ways to make her birdhouses. By rearranging her production process, Gina is now able to build more birdhouses in the same amount of time. She also developed skills that allow her to complete each step in less time. With these improvements, Gina now makes two birdhouses each hour. By increasing her output without an increase in the time she worked, Gina increased her productivity.

Another way to look at productivity is to improve the quality of the output. While increasing the quantity of her output, Gina did not compromise on its quality. In fact, increasing the quantity of output without increasing one's working hours isn't the only way of increasing productivity.

Gina could also increase her productivity by enhancing the quality of her output in the same duration. She could paint the birdhouses with more detail to attract more customers. The qualitative aspect of an output is just as important as its quantitative aspect when it comes to increasing productivity.

Productivity is a measure of economic performance that indicates how efficiently inputs are converted into output.

Growth in productivity is measured in terms of the change in output over time as compared to the change in input over time. Gina could decide that she wants to stop working after she makes three birdhouses. If she produces the same output as before with fewer inputs—such as working fewer hours—then her productivity still increases. Increases in productivity allow Gina to either produce more output or have more free time, improving her standard of living.

Similarly, the standard of living for the country as a whole depends on improvement in overall productivity. Historically, productivity growth has led to higher wages for workers and higher profits for businesses.

This section has six chapters which focus on different aspects of productivity. I understand that productivity means different things to different people and that can also change in different situations. But these mental models will definitely help you better understand your relationship with productivity and take steps towards improving it.

Chapter 1

Work like a lion

A cow grazes food all day.
It operates at low energy
and hence doesn't tire.

A lion works a few hours
but moves tirelessly and with an
absolute focus for those hours.

Each day, lions spend between sixteen and twenty hours relaxing or sleeping. They preserve their energy during the day when it's hot, and become more active at night when it's cooler because they have so few sweat glands.

Simply said, they are aware of the best times to hunt. They don't waste any energy outside of those hours, so when it's time to get down to business, they're refreshed and ready to strike.

So, how does this relate to productivity?

We can all learn about productivity from lions. When it's time to be productive, go all out, and then spend the rest of the day relaxing, assessing, and recharging so that when it's time to be productive again, you're ready to go all out.

As the noted thinker Naval Ravikanth puts it:

> *'You sprint, then you rest, you reassess, and then you try again. And what you end up doing is you build up a marathon of sprints.'*

Essentially, the right approach to creative work can be summed up in four words: sprint, rest, reassess, and iterate.

Most people approach work like cows rather than lions, a trait ingrained in us since the industrial revolution when 'worth' began to be evaluated in time. On Monday morning, you arrive at 8 a.m. At 5 p.m., you go. You have a one-hour lunch break there once in a while. Tuesday is repeated, then Wednesday, and so on.

Instead of working a conventional 40-hour week, you're better off sleeping, pondering, reading, and eventually conserving your energy until you perceive an opportunity. Then you pounce.

Naval Ravikant also said:

'We'd like to view the world as linear, which is, "I'm gonna put in eight hours of work, I'm gonna get back eight hours of output, right?" Doesn't work that way. A guy running the corner grocery store is working just as hard or harder than you and I. How much output is he getting? Outputs are non-linear based on the quality of the work that you put in. The right way to work is like a lion.'

Working hard is crucial, but what you work on when you work on it, and with whom you work are far more important than the amount of time you work. We want to produce new output at a breakneck speed, but if we aren't careful, we will eventually falter, become disheartened, and burn out. This happens regularly, in fact.

We cannot act like we're just cogs in a factory producing widgets. If we work in this manner, we will not receive anything in return that is proportional to what we put in. Outputs are non-linear, as Ravikant demonstrates in that quotation. Work quality is far more crucial. As Naval points out, in terms of creative production, you'd be far better off imitating the lion.

Work less. Rest more.

This book has been two years in the writing. When I started working on the book, I did what everyone does when they start a long, challenging project. I booked my 4am to 7am slot for writing. It went fine—for exactly three days.

The initial adrenaline got me writing two thousand words a day, which is great speed even for experienced writers. But from the fourth day, I was just yawing at a blank screen. My afternoons were groggy and my pen kept drying up. There was no inspiration in my writing, and whatever little I had put together was dry and banal.

I realised that I needed to trust the creative process and have time to laze over my thoughts. I needed to give myself 'resting' time, much like a lion does. Instead, I deliberately ruminated over my thoughts about this book. Instead of putting the pressure of writing a certain number of words, I focused on exposing myself to ideas. I focused on reading and exchanging ideas with people who I respected. I rested actively. And when the time came, I sprinted.

The progress didn't look smooth. There were weeks when, to an outsider, it might have seemed like no progress was made at all. But my thoughts were getting clearer and I was getting surer about the direction of this book and what I wanted to say through it. Over a long enough time period, things actually moved faster and better in quality. Others thought I was stagnant, but actually I was sprinting in spurts.

One might ask what 'sprinting' looks like when it comes to productivity. I think Cal Newport's definition of '*deep work*' provides an excellent framework to help us understand what sprinting for high productivity might look like:

'Deep work refers to activities performed in a state of distraction-free concentration that push your cognitive capabilities to their limit. These efforts create new value, improve your skill, and are hard to replicate.'

Newport contrasts this type of work with shallow work:

> *'Non-cognitively demanding, logistical-style tasks, are often performed while distracted. These efforts tend to not create much new value and are easy to replicate.'*

When I woke up at 4am, I was doing shallow work. We might be able to spend eight to ten hours each day on 'shallow work', but the cognitively demanding type of deep work we're talking about here would be difficult, if not impossible, to accomplish.

Our ability to accomplish this type of work is limited, just like our ability to run all out for an unlimited period of time. Of course, just as with sprinting, the speed and duration will differ from one person to the next. The idea is to figure out how much time you can commit to and then go all out for that amount of time. It's also important to recover once you've completed your sprint for the day. Once I figured this out, I stopped obsessing over time and let the process take its own course. And if you're holding the book in your hands right now, looks like it worked.

Be a lion. Don't try to be a workhorse.

- ◇ Sprint
- ◇ Rest
- ◇ Reassess
- ◇ Iterate

It's your business. It's your life. Why not break the mould and try periods of overt laziness, just like a lion?

Conserve your energy so you can pounce on big opportunities when they arise.

Chapter 2

Time Management

Cheap Dopamine hits are eating
away your day (and your life).

Claim back your time.

Time Management is the single most
important skill we need to learn

1. You are in Control

Before you learn how to manage time, you need to learn something far more important about time. And that is: You own all of your time. At any given moment you are doing what you most want to be doing.

This is a very empowering thought and an eye-opener. Your time is entirely within your control. Right now, you're reading this book because you want to be reading it. If you spent six hours playing video games, it was because that was what you wanted to do. You can't say, 'I don't have the time to work out today'; instead, it was a case of, 'I'm actively choosing not to make the time to work out today.'

So, when it comes to time management, the first step is to recognize that you are always in control of your time. This single mindset change can alter one's outlook towards their life.

Of course, you might have a boss or your parents telling you what to do. But, fundamentally, you are in control of your own time—and you can choose to do whatever you want with that time. If you don't have the time to do something, it's because that is just not a priority for you. That is fine, of course, but don't pretend that the reason you're not doing it is because you genuinely don't have the time.

2. Hell Yeah or No

When we're young and don't have many opportunities, we should say yes to the majority of the opportunities that do come our way. But as soon as you get to a point where you get more opportunities than you have time for, you must start operating with a hell yes or no maxim.

The idea here is that something is either a 'hell yes' or a 'no'. If you get an email asking you to attend a workshop and your reaction is, 'maybe it sounds kind of alright', then your default position should be no. If your reaction was, 'hell yeah', then you should do it. If your calendar is full of things that you *might* want to do, rather than things you absolutely want to do, it will lead to regret because you are not doing what you want to be doing.

So, 'hell yeah or no'. The principle is to learn to say no to things, which is another really important principle of time management.

3. Daily Highlight

Every day, decide on doing *one* thing that will be the highlight of your day. It is the only thing you need to get done that day. Instead of making long to-do lists and getting drowned in them, do just one most urgent, or most satisfying, or most fun task each day. If you do this for a year, you will have done three hundred and sixty-five things each day that made you happy or gratified.

Of course, after finishing this one task, you can do other things, but until your daily highlight is finished, your focus should just be on that one important task. This is one of the best pieces of advice on time management that I have come across and use consistently in my own life.

4. To-Do List

One you have figured out what your daily highlight is, make a list of the other things you need to get done. You can make a list using pen and paper if physically checking things off a list motivates you, or you could make one on your phone or computer. It doesn't really matter what system you use for a list, but there is a general principle of productivity involved here: our brain is for having ideas, not for holding them.

An important reason why we let things slip through the cracks when it comes to managing our time is because we don't write them down. So, anytime you need to do something, write it down in your to-do list and write every task down, no matter how small. This will prevent you from forgetting all the things you need to do and plan your activities accordingly. Finally, as you complete tasks throughout your day, just tick them off the list.

5. Protected Time

Networking is a key part of any career these days, whether you're an entrepreneur, artist, or even a student. As humans, we make connections wherever we go, and even when we don't actually *go* anywhere. You make connections and friends with people all around the internet, and you get to a point where a huge chunk of your day is taken up by Zoom calls, emails and messages. Networking is fine—important, even—but you need to take out some time for yourself each day.

For me, that time is in the morning. I keep my mornings completely free of any obligations. This has been an absolute game-changer, because it means that for at least a solid four hours, I have uninterrupted time when I can do whatever I want. The morning is my protected time for writing.

But even on days when I'm not working on a book, it's genuinely amazing to have some time just to myself. You don't necessarily have to work in your protected time. You can think about and plan your career or you could just choose to relax and read a book or listen to music.

So, in order to manage your time better, you need to figure out what your protected time is. It could be a few hours in the morning or a few hours before your bedtime or just any part of the day. The only condition is that this time should be for you and you alone. No one should be allowed to book into your schedule in your protected time.

6. Delegation

You might say, 'Oh, well, I can't afford to delegate something. I don't have enough money to delegate tasks.' Think of it this way. What is the value of your time in terms of money? How much is your time actually worth? Figure that out.

Say it is $10 an hour. Now, according to the principle of delegation, any work that you can outsource and that would cost you less than $10 an hour, you should delegate to someone else. This frees up your time to do the work that you actually enjoy doing and find meaning in, or is more useful to you. You get to save time for important tasks and someone else gets to make some extra money for it.

7. Choose Satisfaction

The final and the most important tip for time management is choosing to be satisfied with the amount of work you accomplished at the end of the day. When you're trying to be more productive and efficient with your work, it's easy to feel chronically dissatisfied and beat yourself up for not getting enough done.

If you planned to read half a book in one day but you only got around to reading a quarter of it, beating yourself up about it will not increase the number of pages you read. It will only make you feel bad about yourself.

On the other hand, if you appreciate the work you managed to get done and the way you managed your time, you'll be satisfied at the end of the day. And you can plan more effectively for the next day.

Time management is a process; you can't learn it overnight.

Chapter 3
Pareto Principle [80/20 rule]

20% of efforts generate 80%
of the results.

Identifying that 20%
is the challenge.

Vilfredo Pareto was an Italian civil engineer, sociologist, economist, political scientist, and philosopher. Before him, economics was largely a qualitative field in moral philosophy. But he argued that economics needs to have quantitative approach.

He came up with the Pareto Principle while researching income distribution between the rich and the poor. In 1896, he noted that 20% of the pea plants in his garden produced 80% of the healthy pea pods one day. This prompted him to consider the issue of unequal distribution. He considered wealth and determined that only 20% of the population in Italy held 80% of the country's land. He looked at various industries and discovered that only 20% of enterprises were responsible for 80% of production. The generalisation was as follows:

80% of results will come from just 20% of the action.

According to the Pareto principle, around 80% of consequences come from 20% of causes. In other words, a small number of factors have a large impact.

Grasping this concept is crucial since it can assist you in determining which projects to prioritise in order to maximise your productivity. Even though this statement originated from economics, it was later observed that it has far broader applications. Although we will stick to its use in productivity, you will see it in action in many areas around you.

Here are a few instances of the Pareto rule from the professional and business worlds that you might run into:

- 80% of revenues come from just 20% of the clientele. If you work in sales, you might look into the figures and discover that your clientele has this percentage, or something similar.

- 80% of the equity is owned by 20% of the shareholders. Similar to Pareto's initial example of land ownership in Italy, many businesses discover that their most significant investors actually own the great majority of the business.

- 80% of your work is produced during the most productive 20% of the day. The Pareto effect frequently holds true on a smaller scale. You might discover that the majority of your production occurs during those few hours when you're really feeling motivated.

If you're still not persuaded, try running the figures on a few different productivity-related topics—even ones as seemingly unrelated, such as how frequently you clean your apartment or how much time you devote solely to work.

More areas than you'd anticipate use the 80/20 Pareto Principle!

Why does the Pareto Principle matter for productivity?

It's not merely amusing to mention the Pareto Principle at gatherings. It can be an effective technique for increasing your productivity.

We may achieve the majority of the desired results with a great deal less work if we just concentrate on the factors that yield the greatest results.

Yes, it still requires hard work, but you can accomplish your objectives without feeling like you're always bumping into obstacles—which is a feeling we've all experienced when pursuing our objectives. Think about it. We all attempt to concentrate on important things, even if it means disregarding less important ones. You could find that you already utilise this approach to some level.

But it's crucial to understand that you can obtain essential insight about your work by deliberately attempting to apply the idea to all elements of your professional life. Consider these tips on how to apply the 80/20 rule to your situation.

Use of the Pareto Principle for productivity

When you don't have enough time to do everything, using the 80/20 rule at work will help you determine when to let up. Everybody has periods of time when they are busier than normal, so you will need to prioritise what needs to get done and what can wait.

Organizing Your Priorities

Here's an illustration: Consider that in the sales industry, the top 20% of your clients account for 80% of your sales. These are your most valuable clients. When you go to your workplace, you discover that you missed two calls, one from a top-tier client and the other from a less important client. Both calls are important, and both consumers should be taken care of. Who should you contact first?

The prominent client, obviously. If an unforeseen circumstance prevents you from returning both calls immediately, you will have at least contributed to the 20% effort that generates 80% of your income. Although being interrupted in this manner isn't ideal, it happens in the world of business. When managing priorities, the 80/20 Pareto Principle can help you avoid unproductivity when something unexpected comes along.

But it's not just about sales. The 80/20 rule may be applied to productivity involving star clients and key portions of your job, and it works for many other aspects of work as well.

Making a Work Week Plan

Here's another illustration considering your own workday: is there a certain time of day when you're most productive, a period of time when you feel most energised and undistracted? Take on your most difficult and valuable challenges at that moment. You'll accomplish more in that sprint than many people in an 8-hour day if you match the best 20% of your day with the top 20% of your to-do list.

Not everyone has complete control over when they can do their work, but if you do, it's a good idea to schedule your days and weeks of work according to the 80/20 rule. Maybe on Mondays your thoughts are still on the weekend, or maybe Friday afternoons are just about useless to you. Tuesdays and Wednesdays should be set aside for more difficult chores to be completed more efficiently.

Improving the Efficiency of Important Tasks

Another illustration: 20% of the tasks on your to-do list can account for 80% of the entire amount of work you need to do. Maybe doing so entails creating a technology that will simplify other jobs or leading a team to increase efficiency throughout the entire process. Another area where Pareto can be useful is in this one.

Pareto Principle in Action

Friends 80/20:

A person spends most of (80%) of his time with 20% of his friends (close friends) and 20% of his time with 80% of his friends (not many close friends).

To do's 80/20:

The 20% tasks from your to-do list may result in 80% productivity. The simple truth behind this is that everything does not matter equally.

Exams 80/20:

If you prepare 20% of important questions (regarding the paper point of view) then these 20% of questions will give you 80% of the result and for the remaining 20% paper, you will have to prepare 80% questions.

Society 80/20:

You will notice that 80% of the proletariat (the working class of a society) is working for the 20% of the society and vice versa.

Company 80/20:

80% revenue of a company is generated by 20% of its customers, and 80% of customers of the company are responsible for 20% of the company.

Clothes 80/20:

We wear 20% of our clothes 80% of the time, and 80% of our clothes during the other 20%.

Mobile Phone 80/20:

Out of the 80% time we spend on our mobile phones, we spend only 20% of the apps installed and 80% of the apps are used only 20% of the time.

Chapter 4

Inversion Principle

Think about the same problem, but in reverse.

A classic case: people often ask Bezos:
what will change in the business
world in 10 years?

He says: ask, what will NOT change in
the business world in 10 years.

How NOT To Kill a Bunch of Pilots
(as told by Charlie Munger)

Charlie Munger spoke on how inversion helped him as a meteorologist during World War II in his annual address to the Daily Journal Corporation shareholders meeting in 2020. Munger was tasked with creating weather maps during the war. But what he was really doing was authorising pilots to fly.

Charlie said simply:

> *'Let's say I want to murder a lot of pilots. What's the simplest way to do it?'*

He realised there were only two options:

- get the planes into low conditions, causing them to ice up and crash, or

- get the pilot into a situation where he would run out of fuel before landing safely.

Munger steered clear of these two circumstances at all costs. By inverting the dilemma, he improved his meteorology and possibly saved lives.

The process of inversion involves approaching issues from the opposite direction. A problem is turned upside down in order to perceive it from a different angle. Inversion's most potent manifestation is its consideration of the potential dangers of a project and the care taken to avoid them.

According to Charlie Munger, he and Warren Buffett avoided making foolish mistakes, which contributed significantly to their success. The benefit gained by consistently aiming to not be stupid is, incredibly, much more long-term than by attempting to be brilliant.

Inversion has its roots in algebra, where inverting an equation frequently makes it simpler to solve. However, it also applies to non-mathematical issues. For instance, it examines how an investment could fail if you own a long-term position in stocks. What are the possible outcomes that would result in a permanent drop in the company's intrinsic value?

It involves determining what might stop people from purchasing your goods, tuning in to your podcast, or signing up for your email for a commercial or creative initiative. You are better equipped to make choices that avoid those errors when you are more aware of what might go wrong.

Why It's So Hard to Perform an Inversion

Any year that you don't kill off one of your most beloved ideas is wasted time, according to Munger. We all adore our ideas, which is why it's difficult to let go of them. In psychology, there are a few mental models that make inversion challenging.

First of all, people dislike changing their opinions. This cognitive bias is known as the *Inconsistency Avoidance Tendency* by Charlie Munger. You like your choice much more than you did just a few seconds prior to making it. When you find one that you like, you prefer to stick to it because you don't want to be inconsistent in your beliefs, attitudes, and thoughts. This implies that you might not put your best effort into finding any potential drawbacks or weaknesses in your proposal.

Bias created by incentives is the other significant barrier. Once you settle on a concept and have forecast the benefits (incentives) you trace back to that notion, you are motivated to think that the scenario you envisage will definitely occur. You are encouraged to hold onto the ideas you desire to be true. You need to battle this incentive-caused bias and mentally 'give up' on those anticipated rewards in order to change your mind.

Warren Buffett and
His Two Investment Principles

Buffett is renowned for keeping an eye on his investments' potential risks. His two investing tenets are as follows:

'Don't lose money' is the first rule.

Rule two is, 'Remember rule number one.'

He is reversing the issue. He will undoubtedly make some money if he can keep from losing it.

Turn the problem upside down.

The Best Way to Ruin Coca-Cola.

In a discussion titled 'Informal Talk', which was published in Poor Charlie's Almanack, Munger provides another illustration of inversion.

Charlie does a thought experiment in which he describes how you could grow a $2 billion business out of a non-alcoholic beverage like Coca-Cola.

Charlie inverts the issue after going over the 'no-brainer'' inquiries and using simple algebra to determine how it is able to sell so much sugar water (about 3 billion 8-ounce servings per year).

What Charlie believes would kill Coca-Cola is as follows:

- Undesirable aftertaste. You must be able to drink one Coke after another without experiencing any aftertaste issues.

- Losing any component of the brand. 'Peppy Cola' must not exist. Above all else, the Coca-Cola brand needs to be safeguarded.

- Making abrupt or significant flavour changes. Competitors would likely duplicate the old original flavour if you did this and sell it to the irate customers who enjoyed it.

Some of these concepts are based on genuine experiences Coca-Cola had during its ascent to power. For instance, when Pepsi-Cola entered the market, it had to contend with a formidable rival (using half of its name). Coca-Cola also altered its flavour in 1985. 'New Coke' was released and it was a disaster for the company.

The 'Red Team' and Marc Andreesen

The value of these inversion thought experiments isn't limited to Charlie alone. Marc Andreessen, co-founder of Netscape and well-known Silicon Valley investor, has an inversion system for stress-testing investment ideas.

In *Tools of Titans: The Tactics, Routines, and Habits of Billionaires, Icons, and World-Class Performers* by Tim Ferriss, he discusses his method.

Andreessen employs a 'Red Team', which is a group formally created to represent the opposing viewpoint while discussing investments. Marc and his founder make it a point to bash each other; and if, at the end of the session, the defending team is still alive and kicking, the idea is given the go signal. It is a 'disagree and commit' culture, according to Ferriss.

Andreessen believes that examining opposites has merit. He has studied the value-investing principles of renowned investors like Warren Buffett and Seth Klarman, despite the fact that he is a start-up tech investor.

By examining the opposing side of your overall process, you are engaging in another type of inversion.

The Post-Mortem and Failure Prediction

Daniel Kahneman, renowned psychologist and author of *Thinking, Fast and Slow,* endorses the use of an inversion method known as a PreMortem. He discusses the rising popularity of this inversion technique with Shane Parrish on the Farnam Street blog.

A PreMortem is a thought experiment that depicts the fictitious conclusion of your project.

Imagine that the choice you made has proven to be a complete failure two years from now. Your intention is to tell the tale of that catastrophe in writing:

1. *How did it progress?*

2. *What were the main mistakes?*

3. *How did each failure build upon the others?*

A PreMortem flips the debate via narrative. It gives you an excellent list of mistakes to avoid and lets your imagination go wild with potential responses to these questions.

Life's Daily Inversion

I have adapted inversion into my daily life by a mix of genetics and practise. I have a habit of pointing out the flaws in whatever concept we come up with, even when it's my own, which my wife finds to be incredibly aggravating. (Note: It works much better if I offer a solution as well.)

Note that being 'negative' is not the same as inverting. When you are flipping your finest ideas, emotions shouldn't come into play. You arrive at your conclusions about the best course of action using logic and evidence. Just that. Nothing about it is emotive.

You are in a good position to decide whether to pursue or abandon your concept if you have inverted the idea and still have a probabilistic point of view of the outcomes. The beauty of this concept is that it is still a triumph if you give up. You've avoided something that was not as good as it first appeared. The number of good opportunities and alternative actions that you take advantage of has increased.

Warren Buffett puts it:

> *'The difference between successful people and really successful people is that really successful people say no to almost everything.'*

Inversion provides an opportunity to objectively explore the problem by thinking the opposite of what we seek. This form of reverse questioning can help us inquire about our own assumptions and beliefs. We gain an alternative perspective for our question and find answers with greater clarity and understanding.

Our natural mode of thinking looks for answers to queries like these:

1. *What can I do to solve this problem?*

2. *What should I do to achieve this outcome?*

3. *What strategy or process will help me get where I want to be?*

4. *How can I succeed in this project?*

When the solution to what we desire is right in front of us and in confirmation with our belief, it's not natural to think the opposite. Our mind does not seek limitations of our own assumptions unless we put a conscious effort to learn it by inverting the query.

Putting the same questions through inversion model will require us to answer:

1. *What event, behaviour or action can prevent me from solving this problem?*

2. *What event, behaviour or action can prevent me from achieving this outcome?*

3. *What gaps in strategy or process can stop me to get where I want to be?*

4. *How can I fail in this project?*

Applying the Inversion Principle

To apply the inversion principle, start looking at problems and areas you are trying to improve. Then reframe the problem from what you need to start doing to what you should avoid doing.

A few areas to get you started: productivity, sleep, energy, wealth, and happiness.

Productivity

Everyone wants to get more done. But more money has been made selling productivity hacks than anyone has made by using them. Instead of looking for ways to be more productive, make a list of everything you would do to be very unproductive:

1. Sleep poorly

2. Check email often

3. Put off the difficult work

4. Work without a clear plan

5. Keep your phone in your hand

6. Have distracting websites bookmarked

Sleep

Improving the quality of your sleep has tremendous benefits. But sleeping hacks and tricks can be a slippery slope. Instead, think about ways to guarantee a horrible night's sleep:

1. Buy a shitty mattress

2. Stare at a screen before bed

3. Drink caffeine late in the day

4. Eat a big meal right before bed

5. Constantly switch up your bedtime

6. Turn up the temperature in your room

Energy

Managing your energy levels is crucial for building momentum. But, like hacking your sleep, trying to hack your energy levels leads to harm in the long run. Instead, think about things that zap your energy:

1. Sit down all day

2. Spike your blood sugar

3. Get a terrible night's sleep

4. Spend time with people you dislike

5. Work on something you don't enjoy

6. Spend as much time indoors as possible

Wealth

Wealth comes from compounding. When building wealth, it's far more important to avoid ruin than seek gain. Listing ways to guarantee a poor financial situation can be powerful:

1. Gamble

2. Invest without a plan

3. Never audit your spending

4. Spend more than you earn

5. Spend money trying to impress people

6. Think only how to save, not how to earn more

Putting Inversion to use

Master productivity

To take control of your productivity, instead of asking the question, 'What should I do today?' apply inversion and ask, 'What should I stop doing today?' The latter will push you to stop doing inconsequential tasks; this will eventually lead to work that's aligned with your goals and mission.

Manage performance

While considering a person for promotion, people often ask the question, 'What are the reasons to believe that this person is ready to face challenges at the next level?' Now apply inversion and ask, 'What can cause this person to fail at the next level?'

Learning what can cause failure can open our minds to question our own judgement and be conscious of our decision in promoting a person.

Collaboration with peers

It's the difference between asking the question, 'How can I enable better collaboration amongst teams?' and learning by inversion, 'What are the challenges of working with my peers?'

Learning about the various challenges specific to your people and teams can help you in devising a plan that solves these challenges. It enables people to step up in their role and achieve effective team collaboration.

So while the natural tendency is to seek answers to the intuitive question. But there's tremendous learning in applying an inversion mental model to ask the question differently and find answers that don't come naturally to us.

Make an effort to invert, always invert your question.

Chapter 5

The Locksmith Paradox

As the locksmith improves at his craft, the customers become increasingly upset by the lower time input required to deliver a fixed output.

The results are the same, but the perception of value has changed.

The locksmith is penalized for proficiency

Picasso's pick

According to legend, Pablo Picasso was sitting quietly in a park one hot summer day when a woman recognised him, approached him, and demanded that he draw her likeness.

Picasso is reported to have reached for his sketchpad with a smile and created her image with a single pencil stroke.

Taking the paper in her hands, the woman voiced her surprise at how accurately he had caught her essence. She then inquired about the cost.

Picasso said, 'Five thousand francs.'

'That's absurd!' screamed the woman. 'You created my portrait in a matter of seconds.'

'On the contrary,' Picasso replied. 'It took me my entire life.'

I was reminded of this story after reading about a conversation between the writer Dan Ariely and a locksmith.

The locksmith told Ariely that things had been much simpler at the start of his career. People hired him because he was unskilled and took a long time to finish a project. He would even occasionally break their locks. His customers, on the other hand, were always appreciative for his tireless efforts and did not mind paying him for it.

Surprisingly, as the locksmith gained skill and learned how to unlock practically any lock lighting-fast and without causing damage, his customers began to hate paying his rates. They were perplexed as to how something that took so little time and effort could cost so much.

For many people, the locksmith's paradox is an issue. If one considers just the time it takes to complete a task, rather than the time spent gaining the abilities that enable it or the value of the end result, they may object to paying a high price for it.

How do we avoid this trap?

> *A worker's genuine value is greater than their basic ability, and this must be explained to the customer.*

They must explain their genuine value to the customer, which is greater than their basic ability. Successful locksmiths market their responsiveness and dependability as well as their capacity to save you from the uncertainty of being locked out on a cold winter's night.

How do you assess?

Consider the possibility that your computer, containing all of your personal information, shuts down. You take it to the shop, and they tell you that they can completely restore your computer and save all of your files, images, and music for $1000. You'd probably do it without much thought. After you accept, you'll see the technician fix it for about 30 seconds before asking for payment.

How do you feel about that? Maybe you're irritated by how much it cost for the time spent? But why is that? The agreed-upon value and output (computer repair) were met.

> *Is it really important how much time you put in if you get the outcomes you want?*

If you hire someone to do a job and they complete it to your satisfaction, do you care how long it takes, when it's done, or where it's done? I'm not suggesting that you let people work as little as possible, but given that everyone has different attributes, expecting everyone to work in the same way and be equally effective is unreasonable. Companies seek to hire the smartest and brightest employees, but once they're in the role, they're expected to fit the manager's control model rather than play to their strengths.

> ***Look for value in different places
> by letting go of 'fairness' and learning to
> trust one another.***

The desire to treat your staff fairly is only natural. Fairness is frequently evident in the norms that govern how people are expected to work. It's only fair that if person A has to work from the office, so should person B. If person A is required to work for 40 hours, it is only just that person B do the same.

But life isn't always equal or fair, and enforcing justice based on time rather than productivity would do more harm than good. You'll irritate the motivated and productive staff, and everyone will be pushed to do the minimum amount of work in order to 'just get by'.

It's now all about trust. Can you trust that others will execute their jobs correctly without having to keep your 'butt in seat' all the time? If you answer no, there are significant variables at work that are restricting your full potential. Also, you're completely unprepared for the millennial generation. In the workplace, millennials desire flexibility. They don't mind answering emails or working late or on weekends, but they also want the same flexibility during their regular 9–5 hours.

> **'Give your workers a reason to produce their best work every day'**

Everyone works in a unique way and produces their best job in a unique way. Some people prefer the morning, while others prefer the evening; some prefer silence, while others enjoy the rush and excitement of a coffee shop or public space. Does it really matter how people complete their tasks as long as they are completed?

Allowing employees to work to their strengths will motivate them to accomplish their best work for you.

Chapter 6

The Surgeon Mentality

Distraction, fatigue, breaks are some luxuries that surgeons cannot afford.

With someone's literal life in their hands, how do surgeons remain highly focused for hours together?

In most professions, people aren't allowed to work for more than a certain number of hours a day. There are laws to stop people from doing that in most countries. But how are surgeons (one of the most high-stake profession) allowed to work for 24 hours at a stretch some times? And how are they able to perform in a highly focused manner with someone's literal life in their hands?

> **We can learn a lot about productivity and focus from them.**

Here we talk about the surgery to separate conjoined 4-year-old twins. The twins, who shared a body up to the mid-torso, required more than a full day of surgery by a group of surgeons in Utah. How were they able to do that?

A lot of work was done in groups, of course. The separation of the blood arteries, the initial incision, the treatment around the bones, and reconstructive plastic surgery were only a few of the stages that make up a conjoined-twin operation. Of these stages of the surgery, the majority only took a few hours to complete, and a different team of surgeons donned scrubs and entered the operating room for each one.

But in spite of the rotation, the head surgeon did remain the same throughout the procedure. They'd spend as much time as they can in the operation room, with a few interruptions for refreshments and rest. A surgeon who specialised in long-distance surgery said that he ate and drank roughly every seven hours. It truly ws comparable to a marathon, he remarked. 'You must stay hydrated.'

Twins that were conjoined at the head were split apart by surgeons at the Johns Hopkins Children's Center. One pair of doctors was assigned to each twin during the Hopkins conjoined-twin procedure, which had four surgeons operating at once. Every few hours, two nurses would shift into the process, one to each pair of surgeons. Because there were so many people seated at the table, nurses and surgeons who collaborated wore surgical caps with the same colour stripes.

What can we learn from surgeons about productivity and staying focused?

Deep work, as we mentioned earlier, is the ability to focus on a cognitively difficult task without being distracted. This skill enables you to grasp complex material and create superior results in less time. Deep work will improve your skills and give you the sense of true joy that comes with expertise.

In our more competitive twenty-first-century economy, hard work is akin to a superpower. Despite this, most people have lost their ability to think deeply, instead spending their days in a hectic swirl of e-mail and social media, oblivious to the more efficient methods to use their time.

Let's get right to the point: jumping between your inbox, meaningless meetings, and group chat notifications is no way to move ahead in today's information economy. These are indicators of busyness rather than productivity. They won't help you improve your writing skills, learn a programming language, or expand your company. In fact, none of these activities will help you achieve any of the lofty goals you've set for yourself.

Instead, giving in to these attention traps will drive you away from excellence and toward mediocrity. To be truly outstanding at what you do and to be recognised for it, you'll need to take a whole different approach.

In the present and future, excellence won't be achieved by scratching the surface. As information expands and shifts, keeping up involves learning hard things quickly and applying that knowledge to produce work that's exceptional. As Cal Newport puts it:

'The ability to perform deep work is becoming increasingly rare at exactly the same time it is becoming increasingly valuable in our economy. As a consequence, the few who cultivate this skill, and then make it the core of their working life, will thrive.'

We present an actionable guide based directly on Newport's strategies in *Deep Work*. While we fully recommend reading the book in its entirety, this guide distils all of the research and recommendations into a single actionable resource that you can reference again and again as you build your deep work practice.

> *Learn how to integrate deep work into your life in order to execute at a higher level and discover the rewards that come with regularly losing yourself in meaningful work.*

Learn How to Practice Deep Work

Many of us have forgotten how to focus deeply on a single task, or we never really learned to in the first place. In school, you may have done well enough by practicing mostly shallow work on a day-to-day basis, with the occasional deep work session a few times per semester to write a last-minute paper or cram for a final exam. Learning how to practice deep work requires you to be more intentional than you've ever been in sitting down regularly to concentrate on high-impact tasks.

These strategies will help you select your preferred form of deep work, build a routine from scratch, and provide operating principles and tactics for embracing the power of directed focus.

Choose Your Deep Work Strategy

While you may be convinced of the value of deep work, you may be unsure of how to implement it in your life. Newport describes four different types of deep work scheduling. All four of these philosophies have their pros and cons that should be carefully considered.

The Monastic Philosophy of Deep Work Scheduling is the most dedicated form of deep work and involves spending all of your working hours on a singular high-level focus.

While this philosophy has the highest potential for reward and the lowest level of context switching, it's unrealistic for most people who are required to perform various kinds of work in their role. It also blocks the potential for new opportunities as your default response to commitments that arise is, 'no'.

The Bimodal Philosophy of Deep Work Scheduling allows for a high amount of deep work while enabling you to maintain other activities in your life that you find valuable.

Successfully adopting this philosophy requires the flexibility to arrange your year, months, or weeks as you see fit into larger chunks of deep work.

The Rhythmic Philosophy of Deep Work Scheduling is ideal for individuals with a fairly static schedule.

If you can anticipate what most of your days will look like, it's feasible to block off several hours every day for deep work, thereby getting into a daily 'rhythm'.

The rest of your hours are left for shallow work.

The Journalistic Philosophy of Deep Work Scheduling is an option for people who are constantly on the move with little to no regularity to their days.

This method demands vigilance with your time and the keen ability to notice natural ebbs and flows in your day where you may be able to fit in 30 minutes or an hour or two of deep work. Unfortunately, this method is not for beginners and is likely to fail for people who are not experienced in deep work.

Select the deep work philosophy that best suits your work and life. Also, feel free to experiment before you land on a method that finally takes hold in your schedule.

Build a Deep Work Routine

Practicing intention with your time and considering when you'll fit in periods of focus is an important part of succeeding with a deep work habit. Think of location (where), duration (for how long), structure (will your phone be off? Will you break for snack? What about Internet?), and other requirements.

Chapter 7

Parkinson's Law

Work expands to fill the time available for its completion.

Work longer, get less done.

When you establish fixed hours, you find unproductive ways to fill them.

Elon Mus-t work

I have a friend who is a stand-up comedian. He has a peculiar daily schedule, and I've come to know that many stand-up comedians follow similar routines. He wakes up late—around noon or 1pm. He reads articles or watches content all afternoon. In the early evening, he catches up with some friends or goes on dates.

At around 8pm, he gets in work mode and mentally prepares for whatever stage he is climbing every day. To be honest, he is not very sincere about going on stage either; there are whole months when he doesn't.

> *To summarize, he is living in absolute chaos.*

The obvious question that arises is: how does he get anything done with a routine like that? How does he prepare his stand-up comedy special (which is a one-hour performance) when he has no control over his process? What stops him from just lazing away the months without putting anything out?

I asked him this question, and he told me that he books auditoriums for six months in the future. He has no choice but to prepare a one hour special in those six months. If he cancels the venue at a later date, he would face industry embarrassment and monetary loss.

Now, by industry standards, six months is very short for preparing an hour of content. But he throws himself this challenge and his mind adjusts to the timeline automatically. When he has no choice, the work just happens.

I was impressed by this nugget of wisdom. But my friend told me he was not the only one who did this. It was a standard practice that many comedians have followed for decades. Many of them talk about it in their interviews as well.

In fact, it's not just comedians; many performance artists follow this practice. Outside of performance arts, even entrepreneurs like Elon Musk seem to follow the same philosophy. Musk is perhaps the most productive CEO on the planet today, working 100-120 hours a week to change industries and people's perceptions of what is possible. However, Musk likes to set unrealistic timetables. Most people will dismiss this as Musk being overconfident. What they don't realise is that these ridiculous deadlines have a hidden effect known as Parkinson's law.

According to Parkinson's law,

A task's perceived importance and difficulty grow in proportion to the amount of time it takes to do it.

This is why setting deadlines is so effective even if the situation is a little hazy.

Although Parkinson's law is related to procrastination, they are not the same. Parkinson's Law will still apply if I receive the same task one week before the deadline. Also, it only works if your perceived priority is extremely high, which means it won't work for you if you don't give a damn about anything.

Robert Greene, in *Mastery*, said:

'Thomas Edison deliberately talked to the press about his ideas before they were ready. If he dropped the ball or let too much time pass, his reputation would suffer; so his mind would spark into high gear and make it happen at that moment.'

I had an epiphany upon reading it. 'Holy crap, it sounds exactly like Elon Musk!' I said.

Musk places such a high value on his work that he is essentially employing a perpetual Parkinson's Law effect by constantly setting insane deadlines and actually attempting to meet them. As a result of the increased focus, the end product of the shorter deadline is almost always of equal or higher quality.

Parkinson's law is based on the principle of self-interest. Typically, a worker would maximize the time it took to complete a task (or tasks) in order to fill the workday. In the absence of a reward, the tasks would be accomplished more quickly; the resulting time saved would be applied to non-productive activities or leisure.

The principle has been tested a number of times and found to be generally true among non-creative, rote workers.

For creative and internally-motivated workers, the law generally fails.

Student's Syndrome

In my university, it was a widely accepted norm that all assignments will only be done a night before its submission is due. And all exam preparation started around sixteen hours before the exam time.

If I was given a one-month deadline for my final paper in college, I promised myself that I would study the outline in the first week, draft the paper in the second, and conclude it with the third and fourth. Yes, I believed that if I could accomplish this, I would be a model student.

But no, I didn't start until the very final week. And because I procrastinated, Parkinson's Law began to take effect. I didn't want to fail, so I channelled all of my energy and effort into finishing that paper in the time I had left by merely doing the bare minimum, and to top it off I aced the assignment. This is really the story of my entire school career.

In college, my professors adapted to this. They broke down their assignments into smaller portions and frequent submissions. There is definitely some learning there for bosses in the corporate world as well: divide a bigger task into smaller portions to avoid last-minute panic.

This planned procrastination is known as Student Syndrome.

This eliminates any potential safety margins and puts the person under a certain amount of pressure. The term is used to describe this form of procrastination in general, and not only by students.

The Pomodoro Technique

The Pomodoro Technique involves focused work sessions with frequent short breaks. The objective is to boost productivity while simultaneously reducing mental fatigue. This technique uses twenty-five-minute work sessions and five-minute breaks to maximize focus.

The five-step approach to managing your time with the Pomodoro Technique includes:

1. *Create a list of tasks ordered by importance*

2. *Set a timer to 25 minutes*

3. *Work on a task for the duration of the timer*

4. *Take a five-minute break*

5. *After four Pomodoros, take a 15–30-minute break.*

A Pomodoro session takes two full hours, including 20 minutes of break time, followed by a longer break.

Use task management tools

Task management tools help you to organise your workday, schedule personal deadlines, and ensure you have enough time to manage your priorities. You can also make to-do lists and stay on track with projects, whether through team collaboration or for personal projects.

Overcoming Parkinson's Law is essential if you want to take control of your time and increase the amount of work that you're able to complete. If you finish tasks before the deadline, you can use your extra time to get ahead on work or take a break.

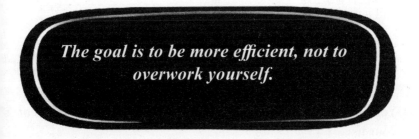

The goal is to be more efficient, not to overwork yourself.

Try timeboxing

Timeboxing is an effective work method that can help you overcome procrastination, recover lost productivity, and focus on the tasks that are most important to you.

Setting a goal to complete a task within a specified time range is known as timeboxing. You become more intentional about your job when you plan how long a task should take before doing it. You can utilise timeboxing to schedule individual tasks, assist your team in becoming more organised, and better manage meetings.

Set self-imposed deadlines

The first step in overcoming Parkinson's Law is to set self-imposed deadlines. Instead of thinking in the 'how much time do I have' mindset, start thinking about how much time you realistically need for each task, and set your own deadlines accordingly.

To figure out the time you actually need for a task, follow these guidelines:

Understand the project requirements: You'll need a broad sense of what is required in order to determine how long you'll need for a project. This involves creating a list of all the subtasks and activities within the larger project.

Prioritise activities and tasks accordingly: Once you have a list of your project requirements, you can prioritise your to-do list and determine which tasks are most important and/or complex. You should place the tasks that take the most time at the top of your list.

Decide who you need to involve: If parts of your project require help from co-workers, you'll need to assess who to involve. Reaching out to your team at the beginning of your project can save you time later on.

Make your time estimates: You should now have a solid understanding of the who, what, and how involved in your upcoming project. You can now make realistic time estimates for completion based on your workload and your personal productivity level.

Think of your tasks as short-term goals the faster you complete them, the more time you'll have for other things.

Chapter 8

Productivity Hacks &
Limiting Thoughts

Hacks make life easier

Productivity doesn't always have to be difficult

Simple hacks can reap big benefits in the long run

The equation to increase productivity involves increasing useful output in less time while having fun in the process.

The emphasis here is on useful output, less time and more fun.

Before learning any productivity hack, it is important to understand what is your purpose for being productive. Keeping that in mind, you can implement some productivity hacks in your life to get the most out of what you are doing.

Two-minutes rule

The idea behind the two-minute rule is that if there is something that you need to do and that something is going to take less than two minutes, then you should do it right now rather than add it to your to-do list.

For instance, if you need to reply to an email or a WhatsApp message, be it work or personal, that actually would take less than two minutes, reply to it instantly instead of postponing it for later. This rule can be applied to any minor task in any aspect of your life.

Two-days rule

The two-day rule is an alternative approach to sticking to your schedule by offering a little leeway.

Do not allow yourself to take off more than one day in a row from any kind of work. If your goal is to improve your health and you need to work out for it, do some kind of physical activity at least every other day.

This allows you to take time off as you need while also keeping you committed to your goal. Most importantly, it prevents you from falling into a slump and neglecting your goals for a long stretch of time.

Five-minute rule

Procrastination is generally a failure in getting started with something but once you have started working, Newton's first law, the law of inertia, kicks in.

If you are procrastinating on a big task or a project, tell yourself that you will only do the task at hand for five minutes. Set a timer for 5 minutes or start a stopwatch and start working.

Your momentum at the end of five minutes carries you on and you end up working for a longer duration. You just need to start and work sincerely for at least five minutes.

Systems

If you are reading this book and want to increase your productivity, you must have a goal in mind. Having a goal is the first step and achieving it is the final step. What lies between the first and the final step are systems.

> *Systems are the process and the things that we do to get to the goal. Focusing on systems is an extremely useful productivity tip.*

It is often the case with people that the magnanimity of the goal intimidates them. You know that you want to achieve a goal and you know you can achieve it. But fixating yourself on just the goal will not help you. Instead, think of the systems you can build, the things you can do right now to achieve the goal at a future point of time.

World-class athletes, authors, or anyone who is really productive always swear by the system of training or the system of practice that they follow. An athlete who is in the Olympics wants to win a gold medal but just having the goal is not enough.

> *The training to win is more important than winning itself.*

Batching

Suppose you have a bunch of similar tasks to complete. The idea behind batching is that you batch them into a single task.

> **Complete it all in one go instead of doing them multiple times throughout the day**

For example, if you have tons of emails, instead of checking your email throughout the day at different times, you check emails all at once, all at the same time. This increases your efficiency and saves up a lot of time.

2x Speed

Listening to things or watching things at speed multiples not only saves up your time but also allows you to consume more media and gain more out of it. If you're listening to a podcast or an audiobook, or watching a YouTube video, play it at 1.5x speed or 2x speed, depending on your comfort.

So if you are listening to an audiobook that is eight hours long, you can finish it in about four to six hours, or even less, depending on the speed you play it at. If you come to a part that is more interesting or a little difficult to grasp, you can slow down and play the audio or video at the normal speed.

Eisenhower Matrix

According to the Eisenhower Matrix, you split up everything you have to do into one of four quadrants, based on whether it is important or not important, and based on whether it is urgent or not urgent.

Based on this division, you can prioritise your work. If something is both important and urgent, you do it immediately. If something is important but not urgent, you schedule it for later.

If something is urgent but not important, you delegate it. Finally, if something is neither important nor urgent, you delete it from your list.

X	Important	Not important
Urgent	Do immediately	Delegate
Not urgent	Schedule for later	Delete

Setting Goals

We have talked about how goals are important. You need to set your goals before you can set out to achieve them. But while setting goals, it is important that your goals be SMART:

> **SMART: Specific, Measurable, Achievable, Realistic, Time-bound.**

You cannot define a system to achieve your goals if they are vague and just there in your mind. Have a clear goal and write it down. Then set out to create a system for achieving it.

Enjoying the Journey

Finally, the ultimate productivity hack is to enjoy the journey. When you're having fun doing the things that you need or want to do, productivity magically takes care of itself; you don't have to motivate yourself.

When you are watching Netflix or hanging out with your friends, you don't need to motivate yourself, because you are having fun. You don't need to worry about distraction and procrastination while doing something you genuinely enjoy.

So, find ways to make sure you enjoy the journey of all the things you have to do. Not only will this increase your productivity but also ensure that you end up having a happier and more fulfilled life.

Chapter 9

Embracing Tech

Technology can be our greatest friend
or the worst enemy -

Being open to adapting and learning new
tools can make our life a lot easier

Technology can be the best productivity buddy

Today, we have access to every kind of information in every form at the tip of our fingers. In fact, there's so much information on the internet that it can easily lead to information overload and overwhelm us. Every day we consume tons of content, of which we like just some.

The problem is that we hardly retain anything of what we consume. Reading an article, listening to a podcast, or watching a video—there's no point if you can't remember the crux of it later on.

> *No matter what you do,*
> *content consumption must be*
> *a part of your daily life.*

No matter what you do, content consumption must be a part of your daily life. Since it plays a crucial role in our lives and our productivity, it is essential to consume content in a way that it can be of use to us later.

To do this, we need to embrace technology. Technology has made our lives easier and tasks have become more manageable. You might not use technology to boost productivity, but your peers and competitors are using it and getting an edge over you. By not embracing technology as a part of your productivity system, you are doing a disservice to yourself.

Technology changes rapidly and new developments are made every day. It may be difficult to keep up with these developments, but that's the best part about it. It helps us stay learners for life. Incorporating technology in your life and goals is not just an option anymore, it is a necessity.

There are multiple websites and software to help you increase your productivity and save you a lot of time and effort. They can be broadly classified into four categories, based on their role in a productivity section.

Categories of software to increase productivity:

1. *Productivity*

2. *Mindful Content Consumption*

3. *File Management*

4. *Communication*

Productivity Tools

Notion

Notion is an app that you can use for just about everything related to productivity.. It can be used for managing your personal as well as professional life.

It is completely free of charge for individual users. You need only pay if you are working with a team.

From taking down quick notes, making lists to setting goals and tracking them, you can boost your productivity with Notion. It also allows you to store links and bookmarks from various websites and apps, all in one place. You can organise your life and track your progress in every field.

Calendar (Category 1)

A calendar is the lash that tells you what you are doing at any given moment of any given day. Most productivity systems in the world just boil down to using a calendar properly.

You can use your calendar to mark out your protected time as well as for time blocking. Another way to use a calendar is to live your life based on calendar invites. If a friend invites you to do something, create a calendar event for it and send them an email invite which they can accept.

> *Ultimately if something is not in your calendar, it must be non-existent.*

This prevents other randomized pointless things from taking up your time. You can use paid calendar apps like Fantastical, or free apps like Calendly and Google Calendar.

Mindful Content Consumption

Kindle

The Kindle device or app allows you to read books. Besides, you can also highlight words or passages on Kindle. This works well with not just the device but on your phone or computer too. The highlight feature helps you to mark out the most interesting or important parts of a book for later reference.

Instapaper or Pocket

Every day, we come across multiple articles on the internet that grab our attention. But we either don't have the time to read them when we see them and they get lost, or if we do read them, they take up the time we set aside for something else.

> *This is why you need a read-it-later app like Instapaper or Pocket*

The idea is that any time you come across an article or a blog post on the internet that you want to read but not immediately, share it to Instapaper. When you have sufficient time to go through these articles, open Instapaper and you can choose to read any of the interesting articles you saved earlier. While reading these articles, you can also highlight text. Additionally, these apps allow you to take notes on the text that you have highlighted. This is a much more effective way of reading articles than just skimming through them in a hurry.

Shortform

Shortform is a book summary web app. It gives you a one pager summary of a book but also detailed chapter summaries, if that's what you want. Along with the summaries, it also has snippets that give you insights from other books that might have similar or opposite ideas or links to websites that prove or disprove the point in the book whose summary you are reading. The summaries on this app are not surface level and they can save your time in deciding which book to pick up next.

Readwise

Readwise, amongst other things, integrates your highlights from various apps including kindle and instapaper. It brings together books, articles, tweets and podcasts. It can save tweets and threads from twitter too. Readwise, then sends you a mail with five highlights that you have saved that surfaced up randomly. This helps you revisit the things you found useful earlier.

File Management

Google Drive

Creating and saving files efficiently is an important part of doing productive work, as is managing them properly. It is essential to have a good file management system so you can easily retrieve any file whenever you need it and store them safely.

Google Drive is perfect for file management. You can upload any type of file to Google Drive and create folders as per your preference to save them. The most convenient part about it is that you can access your files across all devices as long as you have logged into your Google account. You cannot lose your files and you can retrieve them anytime, anywhere.

Evernote

Evernote is an old-fashioned app, but it is really good for using as an archive system to save any letter, any document or note.

You can sort these into categories or you can simply rely on its search feature. It also has an optical character recognition search function, so if you type a word in the search bar, it will show you all files that contain the search term. Whether you have saved photos or text files, the search function works well for both.

Communication

Texts.com

Effective and efficient communication is a prerequisite for productivity. Texts.com is an amazing tool to increase productivity in terms of better communication, although it is best for personal communication. It is a web interface that combines multiple different messaging apps like WhatsApp, iMessage, Twitter DMs, Telegram, etc. You can quickly go through a large number of messages from various platforms.

Slack

Slack is suitable for team communication. It allows you to create channels for different purposes like announcements, general ideas and suggestions, updates etc. A team member can share messages with the other members at once, while also preventing it from getting lost in a stream of messages.

Section 2 –Creativity

We've all read newspaper stories about kids who graduated from high school or college at an exceptionally young age. Some seven-year-olds passed their class twelve exams, while thirteen-year-olds earned a bachelor's degree, and so on. Their parents' chests bulge with pride, and they become the envy of their neighbours.

But have you ever pondered why none of these young children have gone on to become excellent rocket scientists, mathematicians, or even artists? In fact, the majority of people who go on to alter the world as adults were not very gifted as children.

The failure of juvenile prodigies to make it big has been attributed to a number of factors. One is that their abilities are limited to being bookish, and they lack the necessary street smarts to prosper. However, research shows that the majority of prodigies are socially competent enough. The underlying reason is that kids are trained to follow norms, equations, and well-defined routes far too early in life. They lose their ability to come up with new ideas on their own. They learn to accept instructions rather than create them as a result of their early skills and awards. They rise to the top of their organisations, yet few people outside of it know who they are.

The crux of the matter is that early academic success, rewards, recognitions, and even fame, restrict our mental capacity to embrace new lines of thoughts and ideas. Thus, such minds tend to continue tread a path that had been laid long before even they arrived. That is why statistically child prodigies tend to remain relatively unknown outside of their sphere of influence. What could be the reason for this, though? How many such children's prodigies fade away later in life? The following section will give you more information about it.

Chapter 10

Time Billionaires: What it Means to be Truly Wealthy

Time is our most precious asset.

When you're young, you are a "time billionaire"
— rich with time

.Too many people fail to realise the value of
this asset until it is gone.

Treat time as your ultimate currency
—it's all you have and you can never get it back

You're richer than Warren Buffet

Do you want a billion dollars or a billion seconds more?

Because many individuals don't appear to comprehend the distinction between a million and a billion, you'll need to do a bit of mental mathematics before you can answer correctly. One million seconds equals eleven days. A billion seconds is equivalent to 31 years. This means that if you're roughly 20 years old, you only have about 2 billion seconds left.

> *2 billion seconds! That makes you a billionaire in time.*

You certainly don't consider yourself a time billionaire, but bear with me as I explain why this concept is so mind-blowing that it has completely revolutionised my perspective on life.

Let me begin with a query. Would you take Warren Buffett's place as one of the world's wealthiest people if you had the chance? It implies you'd have more than $80 billion, but you'd also be 90 years old. Even though it may appear enticing at first, you rapidly realise how limited your time is in this scenario. The more you think about it, the more apparent the worth of time becomes.

Allow me to pose another question to you. How willing do you think Warren Buffett is to trade places with you and revert to his youth? He'd probably sell everything he owns to get the number of seconds you have left to live. You have something that even the world's wealthiest person can't buy!

You have something vital, whether you're a 50-year-old multi-billionaire or a 20-year-old time billionaire. Make every second matter and don't let it go to waste. In some ways, the time billionaire is wealthier than the world's richest individual.

You can now include
the word 'billionaire' in your bio.
Congratulations, Elon Musk!

The true retirement dream

Otto Von Bismarck made a decision in 1881 that forever transformed the way the world works. Back then, you were almost certainly going to work until you died. He hit upon a solution to youth unemployment by paying old people to just stop working, in order to make place for the following generation. This is how the concept of retirement was born, and it was adopted by every nation in the globe.

This this retirement scheme kicked in when they turned seventy—if they lived that long. The retirement age was almost the same as the life expectancy in Germany then.

People nowadays live well into their eighties, which is far beyond the life expectancy of Bismarck's time. Despite this, we continue to use the same antiquated retirement age. People now retire in large numbers and live leisurely.

What is your time's worth?

Set an inspirational hourly rate for yourself. Imagine your time is worth, say, a thousand dollars an hour. Every time you do something that takes time, think to yourself: Is this worth one grand an hour? Should I keep doing this or switch to something more valuable?

Of course, this is a bit of a drastic approach to really squeeze every ounce of value from your time. But it's an interesting thing to keep in mind every now and then.

Everyone has an implicit value for their time, though they may not think in those terms. Even a billionaire will volunteer to do an extra hour of work if he or she is offered enough money in return (say, $10 million). Likewise, even a desperately poor person will refuse an extra hour of work if the compensation is too small (say, a penny). The value of time can also change dramatically depending on how much of it you have available.

> *You will likely value your free time much more highly if you're very busy than if your schedule is completely clear.*

It's extremely useful to know how you value your own time. If you can figure out how much money each extra hour is worth to you, it'll help you make smarter decisions.

The Greatest Asset

The most valuable resource is time.

Everyone starts out with a little and ends up with nothing, and the longer you live, the more expensive time becomes. A paper billionaire will always wish to exchange places with a time billionaire, no matter where they are.

I had an incredible moment of thankfulness and excitement when the full impact of my being a Time Billionaire struck me. There are just so many seconds left in my life! I don't want to look back at my past and wonder, 'How did I squander time, how did I waste seconds, how did I waste the fact that I'm a time billionaire?' You shouldn't either.

Because they have so much of it, young people overlook time. When you're 22, one day gone means nothing. But what if you looked at your time in the same way you look at your money?

> *How would your life be different*
> *if you saw yourself as a time millionaire?*

Consider this: Every excellent investor leverages their most valuable asset for future gains. Money, experience, contacts, and other assets are examples of assets. Time is a young person's most valuable asset. Even Warren Buffett cannot make an investment that a time billionaire can make.

You have the luxury of planning your life out across several decades. You have the luxury of being patient. Money can be compounded slowly over time. You have so much time that practically any mistake you make may be undone. You have the freedom to pursue your biggest dreams without being influenced by a rushed schedule.

Time billionaires have the ability to make a long-term investment that will pay off in ten to twenty years. When you look at your time horizon in terms of decades, even the tiniest investment now might add up to a lot later since your route is so lengthy.

Critical failure serves no purpose.
You have the ability to care for
both the future and the present.

Here's what you can do

Here are some things to make the most of your time:

Consistency over everything: No matter what you do, if you do it consistently enough for a long period of time, incredible things will happen. Imagine you take a short 20-minute run every day for the next five years. What would that do for your health?

You can be an artist at twenty, a programmer at twenty-five, a designer at thirty, a ball juggler at thirty-five, who knows. Consistency creates great change over time.

> *Do one small thing that pushes the wheel forward every day consistently and let time work for you.*

Outputs over inputs: If you want to do only the things you love to do, you need to disconnect your outputs over inputs.

If you trade time for money, your inputs match your outputs. The only way to make more money is to spend more time. You can only work a set number of hours each day, and you can only earn what you spend time earning. There's no free time, just time that you're not using to make money. In this scenario both your time and money are capped; it's a lose-lose scenario.

In order to change this dynamic, you need to find ways to do great work that increases in value. In other words, you need to make something that's used by a lot of people. You don't get paid for the hours you put in, but for the value you created. That's why you shouldn't look to be paid by the hour.

You shouldn't look to be paid by the hour. Your goal is to be paid for what value you're creating.

Chapter 11

The Creative Process

Creativity and Process sound like oxymorons.

But knowing how other geniuses operate can help us understand our own modus operandi

Being self aware can make us more efficient

Antonio Salieri and Mozart, two remarkable geniuses who lived at the same time, are the subjects of the film *Amadeus*. Antonio was a gifted musician in his own right, but he recognised that he lacked Mozart's brilliance. He became enraged with God because he believed Mozart is undisciplined and unworthy of God's touch. What Antonio failed to realise was that Mozart's father, Leopold Mozart, was a highly educated man who had done his utmost to educate his son.

This raises the question of how much of a 'gift' his son received. There will always be legends about geniuses receiving their greatest works as if they were celestial epiphanies.

> *Every great work, however, is the result of decades of labour.*

Mozart put forth his fair bit of effort. At twenty-eight years, his hands were twisted from rehearsing, performing, and writing with a quill pen. But no one ever mentions that.

As Mozart reportedly wrote to a friend:

> *'It is a mistake to think that my art comes easily to me. I assure you, dear friend, no one has given composing as much thought as I have. There isn't a famous master's music that I haven't diligently studied many times.'*

Mozart approached his work ethic with remarkable earnestness and discipline. This helped him to build a creative process that allowed him to be so productive throughout his life. One must put in a lot of effort in order to build that procedure.

AR Rehman has provided us with a plethora of beautiful songs. Do you honestly believe he came up with them while sitting in his bathtub? Imagine a producer expecting something from him and he tells them, 'I'm waiting for inspiration to strike me.'

He came up with those concepts by actively searching for them. It's worth considering what kind of workplace culture he has. What is the size of his permanent crew and what are their responsibilities? How can he ensure that he has adequate ideas by creating a stimulating atmosphere for himself? When he has a fresh idea, how enthusiastic is he? How long does it take for an idea to become a full-fledged song? Is it the tune or the words that come first? And when he has an idea, does he act on it right away or let it stew in his mind for a while?

> *An artist's creative process is the only true IPR that they own. Each artist has to cultivate a process for themselves via trial-and-error and hard work.*

Many individuals feel that creativity is a one-time event. They assume that if they were asked to come up with ideas on a tight deadline, they would be unable to do it. Many more, on the other hand, have the exact opposite viewpoint. They believe that ideas can flow at whatever rate you want them to, and that if you need to come up with something, you simply do so.

The second group appears to fare better in life than the first.

Neil Gaiman once wrote about constantly being asked the question, 'where do you get your ideas'. This is what he wrote:

In the beginning, I used to tell people the not very funny answers, the flip ones:

From the Idea-of-the-Month Club,' I'd say, or 'From a little ideas shop in Bognor Regis', 'From a dusty old book full of ideas in my basement', or even 'From Pete Atkins.'

(The last is slightly esoteric and needs a little explanation. Pete Atkins is a screenwriter and novelist friend of mine, and we decided a while ago that when asked, I would say that I got them from him, and he'd say he got them from me. It seemed to make sense at the time.)

Then I got tired of the not-very-funny answers, and these days I tell people the truth:

> *'I make them up,'* I tell them.
> *'Out of my head.'*

I doubt anyone who asks really wants a three-hour lecture on the creative process,' he later added.

That creative process is the whole point of this part of the book. From what I understand, this creative process is more of a lifestyle choice instead of something that creative people do in the four hours they spend in their work chairs. The constant hunt for knowledge is an integral part of the creative process.

I'm afraid it is not an exact science. I'm not going to give you a list of things you need to do to build your creative process. But there are guidelines.

Each point here is an idea and a thought, that you need to introspect over and organically build your own process.

How the Process Works

Preparation: The first step is to learn something new. Surrounding yourself with a stimulating atmosphere is critical and doing so is fully within your control. I must emphasise that the mode of stimulation can be anything—attending events, sitting through speeches, reading periodicals, or simply watching movies and TV shows. If a concept is the result of a collision between Ideas A and B, this is the stage at which you acquire new thoughts so that they can clash more frequently.

Incubation: The knowledge you've received is then internalised. You must process and make meaning of whatever has come your way. This necessitates a certain amount of solitude and introspection to polish your inner thoughts.

Illumination: Then there's the *aha*! moment, the 'insight stage,' when two thoughts genuinely do intersect. Many people believe that this is the only stage of the creative process; however, this is incorrect. Although the stage of revelation may just take a few seconds, the entire process can take years.

Evolution: While evolving the concept, a person may or may not wish to accept input. As a writer, I sometimes feel compelled to finish a full draft of a book before letting anybody else see it. When someone does read it, though, I requently receive feedback that aids in the development of my concept. I often gain a deeper understanding of my books by looking at them through the perspective of others.

Elaboration is the final stage. This is where you flesh out your concept and get it ready to go.

A scientist sits at his desk for years, conducting research in order to create something that didn't exist before. When he's finished, he files a patent or trademark application, which becomes his intellectual property. A creative individual digs deep within himself and develops a creative process that leads to the creation of something unique to him.

> *Despite the fact that the technique is not registered with the government, the artist's creative process remains a well-guarded secret.*

Writers are considered to have the strangest quirks. Dan Brown thinks that hanging himself upside down gives him better ideas; he calls it 'inversion therapy'. Victor Hugo is said to have written naked even on the coldest days since it kept him from leaving his house. Others include activities like drinking an excessive amount of coffee, or writing while facing a wall (Francine Prose).

Of course, mine is to check Twitter every twenty seconds, which is the absolute worst thing a writer can do.

Collecting Knowledge

Charles Darwin was twenty-seven years old in 1836. He'd spent years simply studying the world around him, travelling to various ecosystems on land, sea, and air, attempting to make sense of what he's seen. He then travelled over 7,000 kilometres from London to reach the Indian Ocean's eastern reaches. He was standing near a coral environment on the day we're talking about. Damselfish, parrotfish, Napoleon fish, golden anthias eating on planktons, and who knows how many unidentified species.

Charles Darwin had trained to be a doctor but he never took his studies seriously. Instead, in 1831, he opted to join a gentleman named Fitzroy on a five-year expedition (though it was originally planned for only two years) across the Atlantic Ocean and through the southern part of South America, returning via Tahiti and Australia after circumnavigating the globe.

Darwin's methods entailed gathering information by travelling to various locations, reading books, and participating in other people's study, but primarily by just seeing new habitats. In today's world, however, the methods of gathering information can and should be more diverse. The internet, films, and mobiles phones have opened up study areas that Darwin did not have access to. However, it is apparent from his life story that he spent years gathering information and experiences before making his first big contribution to the world.

Organising knowledge –
Working on the Slow Hunch

The idea of a single, defining Eureka moment has been widely romanticised. The Eureka flash creates a wonderful story that is enjoyable to tell. It's been glorified even more in the movies. This is often due to the fact that many brilliant ideas, such as Darwin's, appear to be self-evident.

However, these situations are frequently defined in retrospect, making them appear so. In actuality, they are slowly evolving hunches that take time and knowledge to form. Darwin had plenty of time to organise his thoughts during his long voyage on the ship. In truth, his trip companion, Fitzroy, was most concerned about loneliness and boredom, as his former partner had committed suicide for the same reasons.

Darwin claimed in his autobiography that the theory of natural selection came to him while he was thinking about some literature on population increase. However, a deeper examination of Darwin's notebooks reveals that, long before this insight, he had already developed a very well-thought-out theory of natural selection. Of course, it had taken years for this process to develop.

Tim Berners-Lee, creator of the internet, makes no claims to having had any epiphanies. The Internet arose from an archetypal sluggish hunch. Berners-Lee's concept of using a network to connect individuals took at least a decade to develop.

> *It is impossible to speed up a hunch.*
> *However, if you acquire sufficient knowledge*
> *or spend sufficient time in a stimulating*
> *atmosphere,*
> *you can significantly improve your odds..*

Chance favours the connected mind.

The Aha Moment

This might seem contradictory to the previous point. But I would definitely add this.

> *A ground-breaking idea has multiple aha moments sewn together instead of just one.*

Isaac Newton probably had one of the most historical Eureka moments when he saw an apple fall off a tree. But what is often left out is that he researched for twenty years after that moment before he published his theory of gravity. It took him that long because he needed a lot more aha moments.

A writer gets an idea for a central conflict—this is the aha moment that starts the writing process. But to complete a chapter outline, or the entire book in fact, they need a hundred more ideas.

There are, however, some genuine moments of insight, like this one reported by Albert Einstein, which he got while talking to one of his friends:

'I started the conversation with him in the following way: "Recently I have been working on a difficult problem. Today I come here to battle against that problem with you." We discussed every aspect of this problem. Then suddenly I understood where the key to this problem lay. Next day I came back to him again and said to him, without even saying hello, "Thank you. I've completely solved the problem."

But still, I would not recommend waiting for your aha moment.

Evolution of the Idea

Evolution is an area that a lot of creative people struggle with. Getting an idea is often easier than to develop it into something that will be useful to this world. All of us have a finite amount of time in our days, and ideas need to be organised in order to implement them.

This is where a person indulges in self-criticism and introspection.

A person might ask himself questions like these:

1. *Is my idea really useful enough for the people it is targeted at?*
2. *What aspects of the idea need priority?*
3. *Is it new enough?*

Obtaining feedback is a part of this stage. I've already stated that seeking feedback isn't always the greatest technique, but if you do, be selective in who you listen to.

Darwin may have primarily discussed the evolution of living beings, but the time he spent developing his argument is clearly obvious.

Elaboration of the Idea

There are two ways to carve a sculpture. You can start from nothing and add clay as you go on. This is called the addition method. Or, when you start with rock or a block of wood or whatever material and chisel it down to the shape you like.

Ideas can also work in the same way.

> *The elaboration stage includes*
> *testing and actual work on the concept.*

Late evenings at the office, working at the desk, hours in the studio if you're an artist or laboratory if you're a scientist, and days and nights of testing—these are all part of this stage.

The idea behind sharing this framework for the creative process is to help the reader understand their own process in a better way. It will help you be more aware of your own thoughts and help you plan better the next time you set out on a creative task.

Happy creating.

Chapter 12

The Medici Effect

One way to be more creative is to expose ourselves to an Intersection of Ideas

What happens when a painter meets a musician?

A banker meets a biologist?

An architect meets a chemist?

How the Intersection Point led to Renaissance

In the 14th and 15th centuries, wealthy merchants in the prosperous Florence competed to commission the grandest buildings and finest works of art. Unlike the struggling entrepreneurs of today, artists could focus on their art. The best of artists, painters, sculptors, and builders flocked to the city to debate art in its purest form, thanks to the Medici family.

One of the most significant creative explosions in history occurred as a result of this system, giving rise to the name *Renaissance*, which literally means 'rebirth (of the arts).' This time is often referred to as a cultural movement as it would later cover the entirety of Europe.

> *Innovation involving intersection points of various fields forms the most vibrant environment for creation.*

Multidisciplinary concepts are going to be the most astonishing and ground-breaking ideas of the future, and we will undoubtedly see an increase in such ideas.

This explains why Leonardo Da Vinci is still regarded as one of history's greatest inventors. He was an accomplished painter, sculptor, architect, scientist, mathematician, engineer, biologist, astronomer, botanist, writer, and cartographer.

That's quite the list of accomplishments!

In today's world, no two fields are unconnected. The question is, which areas can you use to spark an explosion of ideas in your school, college, organisation, or personal life? And how would you put those ideas into action?

Galileo is credited with many discoveries, including the discovery of mountains on the moon. Because his telescope lacked the necessary magnification, he relied on the zigzag pattern created by the line separating the bright and dark sections of the moon.

His telescope wasn't particularly unusual, and others had used it before him. But he *was* the only one who had experience, not only in physics and astronomy, but also in painting and drawing. He had taken Chiaroscuro instruction, which is an art discipline that emphasises on the expression of light and shade. This is what allowed the moon's mountains to be identified.

In recent years, it's been recognised that:

> *Breakthrough ideas don't always emerge from experts in a single field. Instead, they emerge when two seemingly unconnected realms collide to create something new.*

It's usually unintended, but there are techniques to make it more likely.

According to a study, fashion designers who have lived and

worked in several countries are more successful. It is not simply the length of time spent overseas, but also the amount of time spent actively working in the sector in that other country. People who had worked in two or three nations seemed to do the greatest work.

The more dissimilar the foreign country was from the home country, the more it aided. As a result, working in Pakistan would not provide as much benefit to an Indian as working in Korea would. The length of time seems to assist as well. The more time a person worked, the better he was able to grasp the nuances of the design sensibility of a foreign country.

Mira Nair was born in the city of Bhubaneshwar, Odisha, which has over 2,000 temples. She remembers seeing travelling folk theatre as a child, typically depicting huge fights between good and evil as it passed through her city. The images of wonderful stories told with constraints convinced her that she wanted to be a performer.

These performances drew tens of thousands of spectators. Mira Nair, on the other hand, was the only one who would go ahead and make films that the rest of the world would see. This was due to the fact that she was the only one having a distinct viewpoint. She was the only one who was willing to be changed by the experience.

She saw an opportunity ticket, an answer to her search for her passion, in what her companion perceived as a half-hour of fun. And it was strong enough to see her through her entire youth, inspiring her to pursue theatre in college after seeing the individuals she had seen at Bhubaneshwar.

Mick Pearce is a well-known architect with a passion for the environment. In Harare, Zimbabwe, he was assigned the unusual task of constructing an office building without air conditioning.

It appeared to be an impossibly difficult assignment. However, his interest in ecology led him to investigate how termites keep their dirt and mud mounds cold.

Are you curious as to how?

To cultivate an important fungus, these termites must maintain a lower temperature. They use a process similar to that of a local desert cooler to do this. The cold mud at the bottom of the mound allows the air to cool. The cooler air is then sent to the rest of the mound, thus cooling the entire tower.

Mick Pearce used a similar model in his building, which won multiple accolades and is the focus of various architectural studies. It also continues to save a lot of money.

Such is the power of ideas colliding.

Guy Theraulaz, an ecologist who studies social insects, met Eric Bonabeau, an R&D Engineer at France Telecom, at a seminar in the United States in the early 1990s. The issue of 'how ants get food' came up as the conversation progressed.

They were both fascinated by how ants determine the quickest path to their goal. Ants function by constantly secreting their pheromone wherever they go. Different ants pursue distinct random pathways in search of food; the faster an art finds food, the quicker he returns. Because of the stronger fragrance, this causes a higher pheromone density along its course, signalling to other ants where the food is.

Guy and Eric realised that this phenomenon had to have broader implications. One of the applications they developed was to assist petrol truck drivers in planning their routes through the Swiss Alps. The goal was to identify the shortest possible path between the fuel stops in the Alps. The large number of trucks and the resulting billions of permutations made the use of an algorithm difficult. At that scale, even computers were unable to provide the finest solutions.

Eric and Guy realised that simulating the ants' behaviour could help them tackle this problem. Eric wondered if he could put it to use at France Telecom. He attempted to apply the ant metaphor to a recurring network issue called routing.

He discovered that routing messages can be enhanced by allowing virtual ants to leave virtual pheromones at network nodes or routers. When he informed his bosses that he wanted to learn more about insects in order to better grasp how networks operated, they thought he was crazy. He quit his job, returned to university, and eventually went on to have incredible success in this field.

Eric established a new study topic called 'Swarm Intelligence' to bring together biologists, computer programmers, and others who were looking for patterns to learn from insects. He went on to uncover dozens of applications for this, eventually launching Icosystem. Factory scheduling, control systems, and telecommunication routing were among the sectors where he discovered applicability.

> *His narrative is a perfect example of a guy overcoming setbacks and daring to create a new environment that enabled the occurrence of an intersection of ideas.*

Few people are aware that Albert Einstein was a passionate sailor. The fact that he didn't know how to swim adds to the intrigue. As someone who does not know how to swim, I can only imagine the courage and craze required to sail deep into the sea with no knowledge of swimming.

He was also renowned for taking excessive risks while sailing. He rented a home on Nassau Point, New York, for the summers of 1938 and 1939, describing it as 'the most exquisite sailing ground I ever experienced.' Residents would have to save him every time he sailed into hazardous waters because he struggled with sailing. The tide carried Einstein towards Europe on one occasion, but he was rescued by two of his pals who took him back to land. According to some reports, he liked to throw unsuspecting scientists into storms just for the pleasure of it.

When it comes to putting ideas into action, one of the most important aspects is to do things that may appear silly if they don't succeed—to take risks, in other words. It entails supporting something that simply exists in the mind. It takes courage to do so.

Of course, things go wrong all the time. It is, however, a necessary element of the procedure.

> *It has been proven in study after study that creative persons are not known to generate superior ideas than others. They're known for having more creative ideas.*

Horta is a small island city in the midst of the Atlantic Ocean, off the coast of Portugal. Because of its position, it became a popular stopping point for sailors from all over the world. As a result, you're struck with the colours, smells, and culture from the time you walk in. A casual stroll down the street will reveal world-traveling sailors in route from the Americas to Europe or the other way around, some from Brazil to Fiji and others from India.

And they're all headed to Peter's Café for a drink.

The café is brimming with international perspectives and ideas. And these thoughts and ideas are colliding on every table, resulting in even more thoughts and ideas.

> *At the crossroads of 'two universes',*
> *real breakthrough ideas emerge.*
> *Two worlds could collide in terms of*
> *ideas, concepts, civilizations, or anything else.*

Peter's café is the ideal location for such encounters. However, they can occur anywhere, and it is our responsibility to ensure that these crossroads occur.

This notion is now employed in all areas of research and development. When a group of astronauts is deployed to space, each one is assigned a particular area of expertise. Architects are now hiring biologists to learn about the interaction between an organism and its environment, and scientists are hiring artists to learn about colour theory.

How can you use this in your work environment?

The intersection of different ideas always leads to unexpected results. But, for this intersection to happen, you need to be open to new opportunities and possibilities and explore different fields. Go to places where you have never been, meet someone whom you usually wouldn't meet or read things that you usually don't read.

Opening up to novelty will lead to creative thoughts and ideas and help you improve in more than one field.

Chapter 13

Free Time as a Call Option

You've incorrectly been told that free time is bad.

The reality: Free time is a call option on future interesting opportunities.

When you have free time, you have the headspace to pursue exciting opportunities.

Free time creates non-linear outcomes.

I've often thought about how to best use our spare time.

During one such musing, I thought that experiences can be divided into 'junk experiences' and others are 'superfoods'.

The 'superfood' activities put you in a state of 'flow'. The American Psychological Association defines it as 'a condition of ideal experience emerging from strong absorption in an enjoyable activity'. If you want to boost your creativity and happiness, you need to choose activities that put you in a state of flow.

According to APA, you can obtain flow when:

1. your abilities are being used

2. you feel motivated, and

3. you aren't self-conscious but rather have a sensation of 'complete control'.

Any joyful activity that actually challenges us has the potential to lead to the elusive flow-state that so many people want.

> *Flow is about being in the present moment and having a great time.*

When determining which types of experiences to put your time and energy in, consider the following seven factors compiled by Wallman, writer of *Time and How to Spend It*:

1. Does it leave you with a story?

Making memories through experiences gives us stories to tell. For example, taking a hike with a friend might lead to a better 'story' than re-watching your favourite TV show alone in your living room. Those stories allow us to develop connections with other people, which provides unity, purpose and meaning in our lives, Wallman says. And when you share a story with someone else, you develop a kinship that increases your happiness.

2. Does it change you?

Anything that forces you to grow or gives you purpose is key to personal development. Activities that teach you new skills or capabilities, change your worldview, lead to epiphanies or move you toward a greater goal, are all 'transformational'. This could be anything from learning a new recipe to taking an improv class.

3. Does it allow you to unplug?

Unplugging from digital devices and notifications when you're relaxing or spending time with others can help you tune into 'real life', Wallman says.

> *'Once you pull your phone out, it instantly pulls you out of being in flow and in the zone.'*

For example, he keeps his phone on silent and leaves an OOO reply on his email that lets people know he may not reply right away. Research also shows that spending 120 minutes a week in nature improves your health and well-being.

4. Does it improve your relationships?

An 80-year long Harvard study showed that relationships, not money, predicted how happy and healthy participants were as they aged. Spending free time with friends and family members, or keeping in touch on the phone, deepens your relationships and also allows you to share your happiness with others.

5. Does it feel challenging?

Leisurely activities should still engage you on a level that allows you to utilize your skills and passions. We are happier when we are fully engaged with something that requires all of our energy. Removing distractions while you complete a task or activity is one way to dial up the intensity.

6. Does it make you feel a sense of awe?

Moments of awe (watching a sunset, spending time with children or visiting monuments) improve your mood and how satisfied you are with your life. Perhaps more importantly, awe can make you appreciate ordinary moments even more.

7. Does it improve your social status?

Human beings care about their social status. Rather than chasing more material possessions or 'keeping up with the Joneses', Wallman says that giving back to your community through volunteering is one way to make your social status more meaningful and make you feel like you're playing an active role in society.

One day a year, spend time alone or with a friend or partner (this works best if you can physically go somewhere peaceful and different from your daily routine).

- Reflect on the previous year and where your time and energies went,

- Set goals for the new year, and

- Determine whether you are closer to achieving what is truly important to you.

Chapter 14

Boredom is your friend

you

Boredom

Since childhood we are taught that boredom is bad.

But experiencing regular periods of boredom
is a competitive advantage.

In the shower, on a walk, at a dinner by yourself.
You're bored, your mind wanders, and
creative insight strikes.

On August 28, 1963, Martin Luther King Jr. was scheduled to deliver a significant speech at the March on Washington for Jobs and Freedom. He planned to demand an end to racism in the United States, as well as civil and economic rights, and he expected a turnout of 2,50,000 people to support civil rights.

He'd known he'd be giving the speech for a while, and given its importance, you'd think he'd prepared it well ahead of time. But at 3 a.m. the night before the event, he was staring at a blank document in front of him. He had reason to be anxious. The night would pass, but his speech would remain unfinished until the morning.

'He worked on it all night, barely sleeping a wink,' King's wife, Coretta, recalled. 'Because his words would be broadcast to millions of people in the United States and around the world on television and radio as the final speaker, it was important that his speech be both motivating and perceptive.'

His speech became known as 'I Have a Dream,' and it is now one of the most well-known declarations in global history.

It's worth noting, though, that the concept of a 'dream' was not included in the original speech.

'Tell 'em about the dream, Martin!' exclaimed Mahalia Jackson, King's favourite gospel singer, eleven minutes into his speech. Although it's impossible to know whether King heard her, he later stated of the incident, 'Just all of a sudden, I decided.' He decided to put his script aside and make a lot of changes on the spot. The speech had grown to be nearly twice as lengthy as the one he had written by the time he finished.

Martin Luther King's approach to the speech must be understood in light of the fact that he was thinking about it the entire time, although he may have actually written it at the last minute.

> *Rather than wasting time, he was practising 'Active Procrastination', in which he allowed his thoughts to evolve into something significant.*

Regardless, he knew how long he could hold off.

His advisors and speech writers were giving him feedback. He didn't decide on a direction or theme for his speech so that they wouldn't be boxed in. He didn't put any restrictions on their thinking and let them travel in whichever direction they pleased. This is how he arrived at the final version.

Great creatives thrive at both planning and procrastinating. They advance in modest steps, getting closer to their goal.

What is Boredom?

We have all had that uneasy feeling inside when there's nothing exciting or amusing to do. You can see it in pets, too. Everyone experiences boredom at some point in their lives, whether it's at work, in class, or simply at home on the sofa.

Unfortunately, boredom has a negative connotation when it comes to sloth.

In reality, boredom is a valuable pastime for boosting the creative mind and so improving one's mental health.

This is true for adults as well as children.

Boredom is caused by a lack of stimulus. It makes the last ten minutes of e-learning feel like an eternity, or as if time has stood still.

Boredom is frequently confused with relaxation, but the two are very different concepts. 'When people have low arousal and there isn't much going on in the world, they often feel comfortable,' says Art Markman, a professor at the University of Texas. 'They have the energy they want to devote to something while their arousal is strong, but they can't find anything compelling.' (Markman, 2019)

This is the main distinction between the two. We, as energetic humans, have a strong need to be engaged at all times, but we frequently struggle to find activities that meet our demands. When we're bored, we tend to go to the cupboard, buy another useless device, or read through our social media page for the tenth time.

This state of mind has a good side that is still being investigated.

When asked for advice for aspiring authors, Neil Gaiman said:

'*You have to let yourself get so bored that your imagination has nothing better to do than invent itself a story.*'

Boredom was so fascinating to the late David Foster Wallace that he wrote a novel on it. He left *The Pale King*, a posthumously released novel, in a tax office and explained his reasoning in a note found with his incomplete book. 'Bliss—a-second-by-second joy and gratitude at the gift of being alive, conscious—lies on the other side of crushing, crushing boredom.'

Consider a period when you were just lounging around doing nothing in particular. Your thoughts may stray to an Austrian field or Alberta's brooks. Your mind also thinks freely, coming up with new ideas that you wouldn't have considered if you were pursuing deadlines.

Leonardo da Vinci started painting the Mona Lisa in 1503. He worked on it on and off, completing it only in 1519. Opinions vary on why he took so long in finishing this one. Some say that he was just procrastinating and being lazy about it, while others believe that he was conducting optical experiments relevant to the painting, which turned out to be important for his originality. Historian William Pannapacker explains:

'Leonardo's studies of how light strikes a sphere, for example, enabled the continuous modelling of the *Mona Lisa* and *St. John the Baptist*. His work in optics might have delayed a project, but his final achievements in painting depended on the experiments. Far from being a distraction—like many of his contemporaries thought—they represent a lifetime of productive brainstorming, a private working out of the ideas on which his more public work depended. If creative procrastination, selectively applied, prevented Leonardo from finishing a few commissions—of minor importance when one is struggling with the inner workings of the cosmos—then only someone who is a complete captive of the modern cult of productive mediocrity could fault him for it.'

One is tempted to believe that his procrastination was justified considering how much he achieved within a single lifetime. He is known to believe that originality cannot be rushed. He noted:

'People of genius sometimes accomplish most when they work the least, for they are thinking out inventions and forming in their minds the perfect idea.'

Boredom and Creativity

What is it about boredom that encourages creative thinking? When we find ourselves being bored, we are often trying to find something to stimulate our minds and fill that void. We typically associate boredom with this feeling of restlessness, when in fact we can see it as a catalyst for action, which can promote our own creativity.

Sandi Mann, a British psychologist, put individuals into two groups in a 2013 study and assigned one of them the tedious task of transcribing numbers from a phone directory. After that, each group was tasked with coming up with as many imaginative applications for a plastic cup as possible. The group that was 'bored' outperformed the others. Another group of students performed even better when they were given the considerably more tedious task of just reading the phone digits.

During a study that was published by the journal *Academy of Management Discoveries,* it was found that people who had gone through a boredom-inducing task—methodically sorting a bowl of beans by colour, one by one—later performed better on an idea-generating task than peers who first completed an interesting craft activity.

The theory is that boredom motivates us to seek out creative outlets to fill the 'gap' that our brain detects. Boredom has the ability to enable our creative thinking by moving us into a state of daydream, which then allows our minds to wander and create without distractions.

But now that we carry an endless stream of entertainment in our pockets, we are almost never left alone with only our thoughts to amuse us. Our imaginations have been replaced by Instagram and our own fantasies by dramas on Netflix.

> *To reclaim our creativity from the stranglehold of our devices, we first need to get comfortable with boredom— both the idea and the reality of it.*

How to be bored the right way

However, while some of us now have more free time (while others are busier than ever), boredom is not the same as having nothing to do. 'When we're bored, two things happen in our minds,' explains John Eastwood, a psychologist at York University in Canada's Boredom Lab. 'The first is what I refer to as a 'want bind': when someone is stuck because they urgently want to accomplish something and yet don't want to do anything that is offered to them. Second, boredom causes your brain power to be depleted. We're itching to put our minds to work. These are the two fundamental aspects of what it means to be bored.'

> *When we encounter the unpleasant nagging of boredom, our initial instinct is to shake it off - quickly.*

It's easy to put a band-aid on boredom with Netflix queues,

Instagram feeds, and TikTok videos vying for our attention.

Noted thinker Mann emphasises the importance of distinguishing between boredom and relaxation. Yoga or meditation, for example, are unlikely to fall under the category of seeking stimulation and failing. She suggests doing something that needs little or no focus, such as walking a familiar path, swimming laps, or simply sitting with your eyes closed and letting your thoughts wander without music or distraction, to feel true boredom.

According to Mann,

It is crucial to unplug at this time. Our culture's fixation with smartphones is destroying our ability to be bored while also preventing us from being truly entertained

'We're trying to swipe and scroll our way out of boredom, but by not allowing our minds to wander and solve our own boredom problems, we're actually making ourselves more prone to boredom,' Mann says, adding that people can become addicted to the constant dopamine hit of new and novel content that phones provide. 'Our boredom tolerance shifts dramatically, and we need to stop being bored more frequently.'

When you're in line at the grocery store, in a long conference, or in a waiting room, resist the urge to scroll. You'll get bored

eventually, and as a result, your intellect, mood, and work performance may all improve.

Boredom and Our Mental Health

Because of our societal attachments to technology, our minds are being overwhelmed with social media, texts, and information. The dual urge to connect with loved ones and go about our daily responsibilities from the safety of our homes has resulted in soaring use of technology. Unfortunately, this implies that our thoughts are constantly bombarded with data, which can lead to stress and sadness.

Taking a break can help our overworked brains relax and relieve stress. Now more than ever, we need to be conscious of how we're feeling and what can affect those feelings. Setting our devices aside to take a few deep breaths can help us quiet the chatter in our heads, and get us to pause, concentrate, and think.

Finding new goals and participating in new hobbies can reduce our stress and concerns and contribute to our happiness.

The Key Takeaway

Allowing ourselves to be bored can provide a little respite from the constant flood of excitement and information that punctuates our daily lives. We must learn to step away from these stressors long enough to become bored and receive the advantages of that boredom. The idea is to strike a balance between intensive labour, in which our brains are completely focused on the task at hand, and purposeful pauses, in which our thoughts are free to relax, roam, and explore.

But how do we go about doing that? Find something to do that isn't particularly mentally stimulating: take a walk down a familiar path, lift some weights, or close your eyes and let your thoughts wander. All of these can assist you in disconnecting from your surroundings, and may provide you with the spark of inspiration or sense of tranquillity you've been looking for.

Chapter 15

Invest Your Time

Each second that ticks by will never come back.

Your time is your only free resource.

Invest it wisely on what matters most.

Where Can You Invest?

1. Invest in 'Life-Extending' Time

Investing time in caring for your health is an obvious example that will certainly yield you more time, quite literally. Days, months, if not years, are tacked on to your life. Yet we often take our health for granted until we experience a wake-up call.

> *Proactively invest your time in your health by eating well, exercising regularly, getting plenty of sleep, and regularly seeing your doctors.*

Invest heartily in those non-physical markers of well-being as well: emotional, mental, and spiritual health. You will reap many hours of well-lived life from them. Learn the habits of the Blue Zone people, from the regions in the world where people live the longest. Some common lifestyle traits they share are: building in natural movement and activity; lowering stress; and being part of a faith-based community.

2. Invest in 'Foundation-Building' Time

There's a little saying that goes, 'a stitch in time saves nine'. Create the time to make the right stitches, and you'll be spared much time, hassle, and expense later. Stephen Covey refers to this concept in *The 7 Habits of Highly Effective People*. According to him, we spend our time primarily on four types of activity:

1. Urgent and important (crisis, deadlines, putting out fires)

2. Non-urgent and important (building relationships, identifying opportunities, prevention, planning)

3. Urgent and non-important (interruptions, phone calls, meetings)

4. Non-urgent and non-important (TV, email, time wasters)

> *Covey says that we spend most of our time in sections One and Four, but the real area of personal growth is in Two.*

If you're spending more time putting out fires than building the right foundations, you'll never get out ahead of your to-do list.

3. Invest in 'Do-Nothing' Time

Americans could use a little dose of 'La Dolce Far Niente'. or 'the sweetness of doing nothing'. something the Italians and many other cultures have mastered. Social psychologist Robert V. Levine, author of *A Geography of Time: On Tempo, Culture, and the Pace of Life* , says that

> *In America, we don't feel like our time is well spent unless we're either producing or consuming. This is a limited (and stressful) perspective.*

In other parts of the world, such as India, it's normal for people to enjoy each other's company without activity or even conversation. Investing in do-nothing time will help us slow down and experience a different pace of life, in which time's value is not measured by its productivity.

4. Invest in 'System-Creating' Time

Making little adjustments to your life pays off massively in happiness, according to happiness psychology studies. Installing a key hook near the door, for example, will save you five minutes every morning searching for your keys. Rearranging your closet so you can see everything means you won't spend twenty minutes every morning deciding what to wear. Devising a better file system for your digital data allows you to decrease your personal administration time in half. Spending some time now to create more structured processes can save you a lot of time later.

5. Invest in 'Cushion' Time

This is one of those small-time investments that may have a huge impact on your life. Researchers John M. Darley and C.

Daniel Batson of Princeton University conducted the famous 'Good Samaritan' study in 1973, in which they placed an injured person in the path of three groups of people to see who would stop and help: those who were late, those who had just enough time, and those who had plenty of time to get to their destination. They also took into account people's religious beliefs.

The findings revealed that religious membership had no bearing on whether or not the person stopped to assist the person, but whether or not the person was in a rush did. Only 10% of those in a hurry stopped to aid the person, but 45% of those in a moderate hurry did, and 63% of those who were not rushing at all did.

> *Being in a hurry may be keeping you from being the kind of person you want to be— the kind who takes the time to help someone in need.*

Including enough of cushion time in your schedule and avoiding 'continuous hurriedness syndrome' are excellent investments in both yourself and others around you.

6. Invest in 'Savouring' Time

Wealthy people are unhappier, according to a 2010 study published in the Association for Psychological Science, because they have a weaker 'savouring capacity': the ability to enhance and prolong positive emotional experiences, such as savouring the colours of a sunset or the flavour of a cool beer. Having access to the nicest things in life may actually limit your ability to enjoy life's minor joys.

It's no accident that savouring necessitates taking things slowly—spending a few additional seconds to appreciate the colours of the leaves, or chewing carefully to appreciate the texture of a mouthful. Spending time savouring all of your day's various sensory moments can ensure that your moments do not pass you by in a dreary haze.

7. Invest in 'Time Assessment' Time

You wouldn't overspend your money if you regularly evaluated how things were going every month, quarter, or year. The same should be true of your time. It's up to you how often you decide to take stock, but a decent strategy might include spending:

1. Five minutes each day to make sure you've completed at least one item on the time investment list.

2. Fifteen minutes per week to reflect on your previous week's schedule and what you wish you had made time for, as well as what time investment brought you the most joy.

3. One hour of quiet time with a diary once a month (or two to three times a season) to reflect on the previous season, how your time felt, and how you'd like to invest your time in the coming season. This can work well with the pacing of the period. Holidays, for example, may imply more time spent with family, the new year may be more focused on work, and summertime may include a significant amount of leisure time.

Chapter 16
Chunking Technique ~
A Culture Away From Yours

Sometimes data points may seem disjointed.

But we may be too close or too far from the situation.

We might need to join the dots or zoom in.

However, the Cherokee people didn't have a script for their language. The bulk of his tribe thought writing was either sorcery, a rare gift, or a ruse. Sequoyah devoted the next twelve years of his life to providing his tribe with a written language, beginning in the year 1809. Incidentally, his friends and neighbours feared he'd gone insane when he left his fields unplanted. His wife mistook what he was doing for black magic and set fire to his first creation.

He began by attempting to assign a symbol to each word in the language, but this proved futile. He then tried to make a character for each of his ideas, but that didn't work either. Then it occurred to him to make a symbol for each word in the language. Within a month, he had broken his language down into 86 characters, some of which were Latin letters that he had learned from a spelling book. The final syllabary was so simple to learn that thousands of Cherokees were able to read it within weeks. Sequoyah is the only individual known to have invented an entirely new written language.

Spending time with a society that was substantially different from his own gave Sequoyah the idea of written language. The cultural confluence of ideas continues to be an important source of creativity.

Chunking refers to the process of taking individual pieces of information.

He took the letters from Latin, took the idea of written language from the US military, and tried several approaches for a written script. He then grouped all these variegated pieces of information into larger units, and eventually, developed a whole new script for a language.

Albert Bandura is one of the world's most well-known psychologists. He is well-known for his work on phobias. One of the many instances he uses is assisting people in overcoming their phobia of snakes.

He'd invite someone who is afraid of snakes and tell them, 'There's a snake in the next room,' which would elicit the inevitable response, 'There's no way I'm going in that room.'

But Bandura did something clever: he broke down the confrontation into manageable steps. He'd start by showing them the snake via a glass and getting them used to it. Then he'd let them stand in the entryway with the door open for a while to get them used to it. After a series of baby steps, the person would soon be wearing a welder's glove and touching the snake.

And, lo and behold, the phobia was gone. When they saw the snake up close, several of them began to like it. As a result, the individual's self-confidence increased in general.

Bandura referred to this as 'Guided Mastery'. It's a method we should employ in order to overcome our fears. It's a variation on a principle I live by: taking small steps forward every day. In the last section we saw the grouping way of chunking. This is an example of ungrouping.

Young Daniel wants his mentor Mr Miyagi to teach him karate in the movie 'The Karate Kid.' Mr Miyagi approves Daniel's request, but the first assignment he assigns him is to wax his automobile in perfect circular motions, which he describes as 'wax on, wax off'. After it has been completed for a sufficient amount of time, Mr Miyagi instructs Daniel to paint his wooden fence in a precise up and down movement. After that, the next duty is to hammer nails into a wall to repair it.

These jobs irritate Daniel because he believes his Guru is using him for trivial things rather than teaching him. He becomes enraged and informs Mr Miyagi that he will no longer do them and that he just wants to learn martial arts. Mr Miyagi confronts Daniel when he hears this, but Daniel's instincts kick in and he defends himself by moving in the same manner he used to wax the car. It is only now that he realises that he has learned the fundamentals of karate through his tasks.

Being in intense attention, being conscious of our thoughts is the building block of gaining ideas, much as Mr Miyagi teaches Daniel the basics of karate.

Suppose there were two rooms with some materials. Your task is to build the best chair you can out of those materials.

Here are the contents of the two rooms:

1. *The first room only has wood and hammer*

2. *The second room has wood, nuts and bolts, a hacksaw, varnish, a hammer and drill*

The obvious choice is that anyone would pick the second room, to make a better chair, to give you more options to work with.

Our minds work in the same way. The knowledge you've accumulated, the experiences you've had, the places you've gone, the people you've spoken to, the books you've read and so on, are the instruments of the mind. Mental tools, like physical tools, enhance our mental powers, allowing us to solve issues and come up with solutions in the modern world.

The more tools you have, the better equipped you will be to solve challenges.
Your mission is to gather as many tools as possible and master them.

The most significant difference between you and Beethoven, Steve Jobs, or anyone else is that they worked so hard to obtain these skills that they were able to generate concepts that ordinary people could not. Pick any genius's story and you'll find thousands of failed attempts for a successful one.

The simplest step is to choose a problem that you care about and go to work on it.

Section 3 –Habits

Anyone who's made an incredibly optimistic of New Year's resolutions knows that very few of them survive the second week of the year.

'I'm never going to change,' you think in resignation, as you break open your sixth can of Coca-Cola. Or, ever optimistic, you might say, 'I'll try again next month.'

Here's a little statistic for you. A study from Duke University in 2006 found that up to 45% of all our daily behaviours are automatic. This means that half of what we do is without conscious thought. The reason is simple: to conserve mental energy. But what does that mean for your productivity?

Let's boil down the working of your brain to layman's terms. It means that your automatic habits are deeply anchored in your basal ganglia (a part of your brain), and they are so strongly rooted they survive even severe brain damage.

Your resolution to quit smoking is going to be tougher than you thought. What's the solution? You've got to get off autopilot and break free of your habit. It's not easy, of course; in a way, your brain is your enemy. Thankfully, there are other parts of your brain that are completely on your side as you attempt to do what is best for your health. In this section, we will discuss strategies to counteract your unhealthy—or just plain unproductive—habits and replace them with more holistic ones.

Chapter 17

Stimulus, Response, Reward

The world today is full of Stimuli

The monkey brain is tuned to Respond

But we can manage the Rewards to break these cycles

When a student has the urge to eat lunch during a class because he is hungry, his response would be to eat his lunch sneakily without getting caught by the teacher. After eating, his hunger is satiated and he feels rewarded. On the other hand, if he gets caught and the teacher scolds the student, the student will feel punished.

In this case, one of two things will happen. If the student believes that the reward is more important or worth the punishment, he will still continue to eat lunch during class. But if the student thinks that the punishment is too harsh for the reward, he will not repeat his actions. Most teachers use this idea to decide the severity of punishments for their students, consciously or unconsciously. Based on the level of pleasure a student gets out of a mischief, teachers punish their students.

B. F. Skinner, an American psychologist, gave a theory on operant conditioning. According to his theory, any stimulus or event that occurs in the environment leads to a response from the individual. The likelihood of the repetition of this response depends on whether, and to what extent, it is rewarded or punished. If a response is rewarded, it will recur more often or always. If it is punished, it will recur less often or never.

Skinner concludes that:

> *Learning is a function of change in overt behaviour. And behaviours are determined by our responses to stimuli.*

Operant conditioning has been applied in various fields. In clinical settings for behaviour modification, in teaching for classroom management and in instructional development for programmed instructions.

We can use operant learning to change or build habits. Any habit that has become a part of our behaviour, whether positive or negative, functions on this model of stimulus–response–reward.

Let's say you go to bed late each night talking to your friends online even though you know you need to wake up early. The reason why you do this is because a message from your friends (stimulus) activates a response of you texting them back. The pleasure you get out of talking to them or socialising online is your reward. This reward leads to the repetition of the response. Even though this might lead to your sleep schedule getting ruined, you waking up late and your efficiency on the next day getting decreased and some health-related issues in the long run, the short-term reward is too good for you to break the cycle.

So how do we break the cycle?

> *You either realise the validity / and seriousness of the punishments / and weigh them against the rewards, / or you create greater rewards for yourself / if you break the cycle.*

For the previous example, you can create rewards for yourself for sleeping and waking up early. You can plan offline meetings with friends during the day since waking up early will give you more time to do things during the day. You can plan a day of efficient work and save time to have fun in a way that not only gives you pleasure but also doesn't make you feel guilty for having fun. Whatever you do, the positive reward should be greater than the negative reward if you want to break a habit.

Building a habit can be easier in comparison since you are starting something from scratch. There is no prior level of reward that you need to beat. If you want to form the habit of reading daily, ask yourself why you want to build this habit. Is it to learn more, for pleasure or to boast in front of your friends and colleagues about the new things you learn? Whatever your objective is, you need to know it and realise how important that objective is for you.

Now, when you start reading or practicing any new habit, at the end of it, remind yourself of why you are doing it or what your progress is. If your progress is enough of an incentive for you to repeat the action, great! But that may not be the case for everyone. Some people need extra incentive/reward. That's fine. You can create rewards for yourself in terms of little treats, indulgence in fun activities or just time for you to rest or take a break. For instance, 'If I read 2 chapters of this book each day, I will treat myself to a healthy snack after reading.'

Operant conditioning tells us that our environment affects our actions and its consequences. But we can modify our environment to bring about a change in ourselves. Whether you are rewarded or punished for an action can be controlled by you, to a large extent. When that is not possible, you can always create greater rewards or punishments to counter the external ones in order to stay on the right track.

Do not unconsciously let external factors affect the habits you are building or breaking.

Consciously take charge of your habits.

Chapter 18
Mindful Action

In computer code, programmers use an 'if-then' approach.

If event A happens, event B is triggered.

We can follow the same approach to build habits.

Specifying 'When, Where and How' of one's goal increases success probability.

Haven't we all tried to learn to play an instrument at some point? We buy an instrument or start watching YouTube tutorials to get the hang of it. But most of us end up not learning to play and the instrument that was bought with great enthusiasm just sits in a corner over the years.

But there are some exceptional people who do actually learn to play an instrument, sometimes more than one. So what is it that makes these people different? How is it that out of two people who bought the same instrument and watched the same tutorials, one becomes a musician and the other doesn't?

There's a simple reason behind it. People who succeed in learning an instrument or building healthy eating habits or writing a book or working out regularly do not just *wish* to do the thing. They plan out when, where and how they are going to do it. The people who set a specific time to dedicate to a skill, and decide where and from what source they will use to learn it, are more likely to actually succeed. On the other hand, someone who just wants to learn a skill but is not mindful of how they are going to learn it is highly likely to fail.

> *Those who create an intention for the implementation of their goals more than double their chances at achieving it.*

Those who create an intention for the implementation of their goals more than double their chances at achieving it.

Mindful action simply means a plan in either of two forms.

1. *'If X, then I will Y!' specifies an anticipated goal-relevant situation X and a goal-directed response Y, that will help achieve the goal. Or,*

2. *'I will X on Y, at Z' where X is a goal relevant situation and Y and Z are the time, place or other conditions suitable for the goal.*

It is a strategy that you can follow through to achieve your goals down to the last detail.

The Psychology of Mindful Action

Mindful actions are performed by a conscious act of will.

Their effects, however, come about by automatic action control.

The first component of mindful action is specifying an anticipated critical situation or desired condition, like a sunny morning or one hour of free time in the evening. This serves to heighten the activation of its mental representation. For instance, sunny mornings are more noticeable to you, or you have time at 5 p.m. to practice guitar. As a consequence, the critical situation is more easily recognized, more readily attended to, and more effectively recalled.

Mindful actions facilitate goal pursuit by making the planned response (the act of practicing guitar, here) automatic in response to that critical situation. Once a link is formed between the anticipated critical situation and the goal-directed response, the individual encountering the situation is able to enact the response without a second act of conscious will.

Problems That Mindful Action Solves

Getting Started

The first problem with goals is that once a goal has been set, people fail to initiate goal-directed responses when given the opportunity.

There are a number of reasons for this:

1. individuals may fail to notice an opportunity to get started on the pursuit of their goal

2. they may be unsure of how they should act when the moment presents itself

3. or they may simply forget about their goal when busy with other things.

> *Mindful action makes the critical situation easier to notice and the response easier to perform.*

It reduces this problem of getting started on one's goals even when busy with other activities.

Distractions

Individuals may also get derailed from a goal-directed course of action. Because many goal pursuits entail continuous striving and repeated behavioural performances, goal pursuit from be shielded from distractions. These distractions can come in the form of temptations and moods that can unknowingly affect one's ability to succeed.

Mindful actions can protect goal pursuit from unwanted habits in favour of a newly set goal.

Over-extending The Self

Individuals who expend effort on a given goal pursuit experience a subsequent reduction in the ability to self-regulate. This is called ego depletion. It results from having drained one's regulatory resources by exercising self-control in a demanding first task. The ego-depleted individual then shows lowered performance in a subsequent task.

Because mindful actions make self-regulation more automatic, they can be used to prevent the emergence of ego depletion and to enhance performance once ego depletion has occurred.

Rigidity

There are times when flexibility in goal pursuit is required. Perhaps new information changes the goal's value and it ought to be abandoned. Perhaps the method of approaching the goal is ineffective and needs alteration. In such situations, rigidity might result in a failure to achieve one's goal.

Research has shown that there are a number of ways that mindful actions combat rigidity. Goal pursuit by mindful actions respects the quality of the final goal. Specifying a good opportunity to act on one's mindful action does not make a person oblivious to better alternative opportunities

> *Goal pursuit by mindful actions respects the quality of the final goal. It does not make a person unresponsive to the ineffectiveness of their plans.*

So it can be used to disrupt the escalation of commitment. When one course of action doesn't work, they can abandon it and follow a new one.

To make mindful action easier, you can track your new habits on regular intervals by recording the plan you made to implement the intention and the success rate of that plan in a short duration. This makes it easier to notice when an intention has truly become your habit and change plans as soon as you notice the ineffectiveness of your original plans. You can use either a physical or a digital habit tracker for this purpose.

If you want to journal daily, don't plan to do it every day *if* you find time for it. You're not going to find the time if you take this approach! Instead, plan ahead and tell yourself, 'I will spend 15 minutes journaling my thoughts tomorrow morning, right after I wake up.' Of course, you can decide the conditions for your mindful action based on what is suitable for you and the effectiveness of those conditions.

Mindful action increases your success rate in building a good habit or breaking a bad one, even if it doesn't necessarily make the process any easier.

Chapter 19
Gaming Your Mind

Much like a building, habits can be built on top of each other

The foundation of an existing habit can be used to build storeys of new habits on it

Forming a new habit requires a change in your behaviour. Behaviour change is tricky. It hurts, needs discipline and there are no shortcuts. This is why making a new habit stick is so difficult. But there are ways to make behavioural changes more convenient and new habits easier to inculcate. The technique we are talking about is *habit stacking*.

The idea behind habit stacking is that by clustering the habits we want to develop and sustain, we stand a better chance of remembering them by associating related tasks with each other—hence clustering or 'stacking' new behaviours.

> *Habit stacking allows you to organise these habits in a way that makes logical sense for the way your day works already*

You instead change micro-habits, one stack or cluster at a time.

You start by looking at all the things you want to include and organising them sensibly and logically. You break down your day into chunks, e.g., morning routine, commute, lunchtime, evening, bedtime. Then you stack the behaviours you want to introduce by associating them with morning rituals, night routines, etc.

Let's take the example of journaling from the last chapter.

Say you want to journal every morning, and you want to eat a healthy breakfast along with the coffee you already have. Habit stacking would require you to keep your journal near your bed, so the first thing you see after waking up is your journal and you act on your decision to journal.

Alternatively, you could also stack it with your habit of drinking coffee. Place your journal on your coffee table so you link coffee with journaling. Make preparations for your breakfast the night before, or place your breakfast on the counter or in the front shelves, so you notice it when you enter your kitchen to make coffee. You will start associating journaling and healthy breakfast with waking up and coffee. These new habits will not slip your mind, and with some effort, you will actually start following them.

As another example, people who spend a significant amount of time on public transport can use their commute time for journaling or listening to a podcast instead of just scrolling through social media.

> *Practice your routine for some time even if you find that it takes a lot of effort to stick to it.*

Eventually your mind will form a link between things like waking up or morning coffee or commuting and the new habits that you want to build. The new habit will come automatically to you and you won't have to remind yourself to do it.

Information processing happens in the prefrontal cortex of our brain. It requires a lot of energy to use this part of the brain; this is why it is so difficult to stick to new habits in the beginning. But in about a month or two, the information shifts to another part of the brain where more automatic behaviour patterns are stored. The effort becomes less, the tasks get more natural and you make your way to long lasting behaviour changes.

Habit Stacking Tips

Don't do it all at once

Focus on different areas of your day or life, one at a time. Trying to change everything at once can get overwhelming and become counterproductive.

Have a solid anchor

Make sure that you already practice the habit around which you are stacking other new habits. For example, you can only journal in the morning if you actually wake up in the morning with enough time to spare. So make sure that you are already an early bird or you won't be able to follow your morning ritual.

Start small

Don't try to become a pro at your habit in just one day. If you want to start journaling, start with a few minutes a day.

You can use journal prompts if you don't know where to start journaling. Slowly make your way to spending more time on journaling or finding your own creative ways to journal.

Repeat

You cannot expect your brain to solidify your new habits in a day or two. Repeat the routine you have made for a few weeks and give your brain time to associate and automate new habits into behaviour patterns.

As a writer, it is essential for me to work on my ideas and write something every day even if I don't particularly like what I write. Earlier, on days when I had no motivation to write or I felt like I didn't have any good ideas to work on, I found it hard to get myself to sit and write.

Habit stacking has helped me a lot with this problem. I know that whether I have motivation or not, I always have four hours in the morning to myself. I started keeping my laptop, notebook and pens near my bed so that as soon as I woke up, I couldn't ignore my commitment to writing. I carry a notebook with me wherever I go so that I don't waste any spare time or I don't let an idea slip through my mind because I didn't note it when I got it.

Practicing habit stacking has been one of the best decisions for my writing and it is now impossible for me to go a day without writing at least one page even if I don't feel motivated enough. This is useful because later when I read these pages, I either realise that I did have a good idea or at least I realise the loopholes in my writing and can improve upon it.

> *Habit stacking is basically about building new habits by taking advantage of the old ones.*

It is especially useful because you can change not just one but a cluster of habits at a time. This helps you to change significantly in a shorter time rather than taking time to change one habit at a time. It increases your productivity in building a new lifestyle and changing yourself for the better.

Much like habit stacking, there's another way of gaming your mind. We often believe that in order to change our habits, achieve our goals or produce more, we need to increase our motivation and willpower. Although they might help you to get started, there is another element that seems to be even more effective: purposefully designing our environment. Changing your habits is easy if you actively take steps to trick your mind. The idea that our environment directly affects our actions is not a radical one.

> *In order to tame your mind, you need to game your mind.*

In order to understand how we can game our mind, let's first understand the concept of choice architecture. We are not as rational as we think: our decision-making capacities are often victims of a number of cognitive biases and errors. The number of choices presented, the way in which they are presented to us, and even the presence of a 'default', can influence what we choose to consume. This concept is used as a marketing strategy by many stores across the world. The objective of choice architecture, in that context, is to designing the environment so that automatic cognitive processes push us to make more favourable choices.

The dairy section has the highest conversion rate; there are very few people that look at milk and not buy it. This section, contrary to what you might think is the logical place to position it, is usually located at the *back* of the supermarket. This is intentionally done in order to pull the shopper as deeply into the store as possible. On your way to getting the milk, you walk through the middle of the store where the tougher-to-sell items are displayed. These items might not have been on your shopping list, but once you see them on the shelves, you get attracted and your cart triples in size.

Just as supermarkets trick you into buying things you don't need, you can trick your mind into doing things it doesn't want to do. You may not be able to control the environment in a supermarket, but you can control the environment at your home.

If your goal is to eat healthy, you can choose not to store unhealthy snacks at your home. You can also store healthy snacks in a way that makes it easier for you to see them when you enter the kitchen or open the refrigerator. Avoiding junk food is harder if it's is the first thing you see when you enter the kitchen.

> ***Control your environment.
> Make the habits you want to break
> more difficult to act upon.***

All of our habits and recurring activities start with a cue— an image, a sound, or even a smell. Most people let the circumstances and their environment affect their daily life, but we can always choose not to. By increasing positive cues and eliminating negative ones, you can take back control of your life, even if it is done subconsciously.

A 2004 study found that if people have to opt-in to donate organs, many stick with the default option of not opting in. But, if you have to opt-out, many more will become donors. Donor registration rates were twice as high when potential donors had to opt out instead of opting into donor registration.

Vaccinations are very beneficial if everyone takes them but many people do not bother to get vaccinated. But when vaccination drives are held in schools and every student has to get vaccinated unless someone's parents object, students are much more likely to get vaccinated and vaccination rates increase significantly.

If your phone is placed right beside your bed, you will be tempted to use it the first thing in the morning. But if placed in another corner of the room or in a different room altogether, the chances of scrolling through it reduce drastically.

Section 4 – Learning

Learning is the mental exercise that our brain needs.

Learning is usually enjoyable at first but becomes tedious after a time. Let's look at what happens when you try to master a new skill. Take, for example, learning robotics, which I did during my freshman year of college.

Stage 1 – Unconscious incompetence – Being the cocky dude that I am, I look at most things and say 'Eh, this looks easy.' Robotics was no exception. Surely everything was on the internet these days (although it *was* 2005), and all I needed were some wires and motors and all that. I narrowed down on a project: build a line follower, or a wheeled robot (sort of like a toy car), which would autonomously follow a black line on a white surface on the ground.

Of course, despite my naïve enthusiasm, it didn't take me very long to realise I was wrong.

Stage 2 – Conscious incompetence – The time when you truly grasp the difficulty of mastering your new interest is possibly the hardest stage. I started reading the material and realised that the content was in a language completely different from anything I could comprehend. It inevitably dawned on me that making this robot would take a lot more effort and time than I had initially planned. I began doubting whether I was cut out for this or not. This is the stage at which most people give up.

I decided to put everything else in my life (not that I had much at 19 years of age!) on hold and concentrate on this.

Stage 3 – Conscious competence – As I stuck with it, the strongest memory I have of that period is of losing eight kilograms in two months as I struggled day in day out with solders, circuits, motors and sensors. In the end, I managed to make a functioning Line Follower, which went on to win a few college competitions as well. This was the first and the only time I would come close to becoming a college celebrity.

I was gratified, of course, but I was aware that I had a long way to go in the world of robotics.

Stage 4 – Unconscious competence – This is the time when you start to reap the rewards of your hard work. Despite the fact that my talent in robotics led to a paid internship in Paris at the age of twenty, I would argue that I did not reach this stage. After graduation, I gave up robotics and followed a different path.

It's easiest to tell if you're in the unconscious competence stage by comparing it to driving. When you've been driving for a while, it's common to lose track of your activities since you were entirely absorbed in your thoughts. That was not the case when you first started driving.

Chapter 20

The Feynman Technique

To learn anything:

Step 1: Identify a topic

Step 2: Try to explain it to a 5-year-old

Step 3: Study to fill in knowledge gaps

Step 4: Organize, convey, and review

True genius is the ability to simplify, not complicate.

Charlie Munger shared a fascinating but fictional anecdote about two persons in a 2007 graduation speech: the brilliant physicist Max Planck and his valet. Max was unquestionably an astute scientist. Germans loved to hear him. With his chauffeur, he travelled around the country giving presentations about his job.

The chauffeur was bored of hearing the same speech over and over again day after day. Finally, he inquired: 'Can I give the speech this time, Max? I've heard that so many times that I've memorised it.' Max consented to the chauffeur delivering the speech. He sat in the front row and donned the chauffeur's cap. The chauffeur pretended to be Max and did an excellent job. The speech went off without a hitch.

A tiny man stood up at the conclusion and asked the chauffeur a question. What was his response?

'I'm shocked you asked that question; it's such a straightforward one. Even my driver can answer this.'

The tale shows the contrast between two types of information: deep knowledge, which Max possessed, and shallow knowledge, which the chauffeur possessed.

> *There is an abundance of information in our world. However, a select few go beyond the surface to have a thorough understanding of the subject and hence possess profound knowledge.*

What is The Feynman Technique?

In short, it's a simple approach to *self-directed learning* that is based on distilling what you know. Albert Einstein is often credited with having said that you don't know something well if you can't explain it to a child. That's the Feynman Technique in a nutshell.

The technique is named after Richard Feynman, an American theoretical physicist who, among his other efforts, was involved in the Manhattan Project. He had a background in doing exactly what you might expect: teaching himself complicated ideas, like quantum computing and particle physics, and nanotechnology. His ability to translate complex scientific theories into more accessible terms earned him the title of 'the great explainer'.

> *There are two main goals to strive for when using the Feynman Technique: be simple and concise.*

See if you can explain the concept to a five-year-old. If you can, try to come up with an original analogy to help you explain the topic.

Creating an analogy is a fantastic way to gain mastery over an idea and learn empathy. It forces you to meet the person at their level of understanding and teach them something new by relating it to an idea they're already familiar with.

How to use the Feynman Technique?

1. Clarify exactly what you want to learn

Clarify the concept you want to understand and write it at the top of a blank piece of paper. The more specific you are, the cleaner and more efficient the rest of the learning process can be.

2. State (and self-assess) current understanding

In the plainest language possible, write down an explanation of the idea as if you were teaching it to someone who does not understand it at all. You can start out with a broad summary and then get more specific, working through examples, scenarios, or other subtleties of the concept. Simply stating it broadly isn't enough to fully demonstrate 'understanding', but rather works as a foothold to work from as you demonstrate that understanding.

3. Acquire new knowledge

What is the Feynman Technique? In the broadest possible sense, it's about acquiring new knowledge. You are attempting to exhibit a more or less complete comprehension of the material you're learning with both accuracy and precision. If you can't explain it fully, go back and relearn your source material until you are more confident.

If we lack expertise, it can be difficult to know what we do know or don't know; this technique isn't perfect. However, as you become accustomed to the technique–and self-directed learning in general–you can develop a better instinct for what concepts you don't understand and how to go about increasing your understanding.

4. Document new knowledge and clarify new understanding

Reflect on and document new knowledge as you obtain it, especially how your understanding has changed. It is a good idea to use visualisations, concept maps, and various forms of analogies to clarify your own thinking. Your display of that understanding should adapt as your understanding evolves. This will both broaden your knowledge of the subject and shed light on the learning process (which can carry over into learning about new topics).

5. Restate evolved understanding (i.e., as compared to step 2)

Once you've 'done the work' of learning, try to–without checking your paper or other research notes or documentation–state your understanding again–from scratch and without reference. If you can't, go back and repeat steps 3 through 5.

How I Mastered Learning

Now I'll tell you about a time during my college years when I had an exam coming up and was certain I'd fail because I had slacked off the previous year. But I wasn't going to give up, so I promised everyone that the day before the exam, I'd clear up any questions they had. Not only did I prepare well theoretically, but I also broke down the challenges like a 6-year-old might.

I exceeded the rest of the class because I had thoroughly prepared for the paper—and it was all thanks to Feynman's Technique, which enabled me to restate what I'd learnt by resolving my doubts.

Since then, I've been employing the method to learn any new topic or idea. It stays with me indefinitely rather than for a short length of time in this fashion. And now that you know how it can help you, go ahead and learn something new today.

Any intelligent fool can make things bigger, more complex, and more violent. It takes a touch of genius—and a lot of courage—to move in the opposite direction.

— E.F. Schumacher

Chapter 21
Intellectual Sparring
Partners

Most of us need fewer friends and more intellectual sparring partners.

Friends are easy to come by.

Intellectual sparring partners are harder to find.

They will call you on your BS, question your assumptions, and push you to think deeply.

We've all heard of Freddie Mercury, the lead singer of the music band *Queen*. A casual glance of his life might reveal an accomplished singer, but Freddie had had his share of difficulties when his band mates abandoned him following a fight. He quickly replaced them with others, but the quality of his music suffered as a result.

He explained that when he told his new friends to do something, they simply did it. For his best work to emerge, he needed to be challenged. He needed to spar in order to do his job. This sparring allows one to test their limitations and learn more than what is offered to them.

> *One approach to do so on a regular basis*
> *would be to surround ourselves*
> *with intellectual sparring partners who would*
> *challenge us without disrupting our flow.*

What exactly is an intellectual sparring partner? It could be a friend, co-worker, or acquaintance with the background, competency, and personality to assist you enhance the quality of your reasoning and decision-making through active, grounded conversation and dispute. Regular 'sparring sessions' — one hour on a predetermined weekly or monthly cycle, with specific topics and expected outcomes to guide the debate — will aid in the establishment of structure. This will not only help you study more, but it will also give you a sense of personal improvement.

Having a sparring partner is essential for your personal growth.

I was once tasked with writing an article about AI. I understood very little about the issue at that point, but there was no way I was going to give up. Suddenly, it occurred to me that I may seek assistance from a close friend. Because we were both familiar with each other's working style and routines, he could help me get things done flawlessly. We had become each other's intellectual sparring partners, if you will. He had a wealth of information up his sleeve that he would reveal when I least expected it, assisting me in learning new things every time I was in his presence.

Today, the piece is widely regarded as one of my best works, with readers and critics alike praising it. And I wouldn't have been able to do it without the help of my cerebral sparring buddy.

Take a look at you now.

Examine the people you regularly meet to see if they assist you improve in the same way that an intellectual sparring partner would.

How to Identify an Intellectual Sparring Partner?

Let's shift to the tactical: how can you identify your intellectual sparring partner? First off, it's important to note that there is no such thing as a one-size-fits-all intellectual sparring partner. The person that works for me might not work for you, and vice versa.

Here are a few of the traits to consider in identifying yours:

- *Background: Different from your own across a number of vectors. A fundamentally different 'map of reality' is ideal.*

- *Competency: Exhibited clarity and depth of thinking; an analytical mind that is able to deconstruct problems into component parts.*

- *Personality: Kind. You need to feel safe with the person and know that they operate from a basic stance of kindness. But it is essential that this kindness must not interfere with their willingness to be direct.*

Start by thinking about the existing relationships in your life. You might find that there are a few candidates in that pool that fulfil the above criteria. If not, keep looking. This person (or group of people) will play an important role in your life. There's no need to stop at one—you might find that having different sparring partners for personal and professional matters is useful.

We need to be challenged to grow. We must push our boundaries beyond the usual so we could see what lies outside our possibilities. Whoever your intellectual partner is, make sure they are:

- Someone who doesn't work with you

- Someone who isn't afraid to push back

- Someone who has complementary superpowers to you

- Someone who is invested in your success

Chapter 22
10/10/10 Principle

We're all guilty of making decisions without thinking about long term consequences.

To avoid this, ask:
- How will I feel about this ten minutes from now?

- Ten months from now?

- Ten years from now?

This helps clarify the decision that results in a win/win/win.

Every day, you make tons of decisions. Is scrambled eggs on the menu? Should I go to the gym or stay home? Should I ask her out? Is it acceptable for me to ask for a raise?

Your decisions have an impact on your life. Your career path is mostly decided by the job you select. Your health is influenced by the foods you consume. The city you live in and the apartment you live in have a big impact on your standard of living.

How many times have you wished you hadn't made a decision? Have you squandered a significant amount of time, money, and effort as a result of that decision? Perhaps the job turned out to be a dead end; the partner is a jerk but you still choose to stay; the high-risk investment has failed. Consider how your life may be different if you'd made better decisions. You'd have a lot more of what you want, and far less of what you don't want.

However, why do we make decisions that we subsequently regret? And how can we make them better?

Making Better Decisions with the 10–10–10 Rule

Making better decisions isn't actually that hard. You simply have to think about the rational long-term consequences instead of being absorbed by short-term emotions.

The 10–10–10 rule will help you do that. When you face a difficult decision, you split it into three parts. You ask yourself:

> *How will I feel about this in*
> *ten minutes, ten months,*
> *and ten years from now?*

It's as simple as it is effective.

These three timelines are unusual in that they allow you to assess your choice from three different angles. They give you a well-balanced, comprehensive, and realistic picture of how your choice will play out.

Your emotions will still determine how you feel about it in 10 minutes. It's a good starting point for figuring out how you feel about the situation right now.

Your choices might have a major, albeit different, impact on you in ten months. Your short-term emotions have dissipated, and the mid to long-term effects of your action have manifested themselves in your life.

Your decision will be either entirely meaningless or potentially life-altering in ten years, with very nothing in between. It's a smart method to assess the long-term implications of a decision instead of spending weeks debating it.

Putting it into practice

During my undergraduate years, my roommate and I had a terrific friendship; but living together had its drawbacks. There were a number of subjects where we may have differed. Cleaning and dishwashing are merely the tip of the iceberg when it comes to household chores. Things rapidly deteriorated despite a chat and some temporary improvement.

I was disappointed, enraged, and resentful at first. I pondered approaching him again, but I was certain it would be a pointless effort. But then I made the decision to take matters into my own hands and choose 10–10–10. This is how I came up with the idea to try again.

In ten minutes, I'd be miserable since I was still be in a state of mental upheaval and wouldn't even dream of talking to him.

But in ten months, I'd be glad I tried to save my friendship with one of my best friends. Regardless of the outcome, I would regret not taking the shot now.

In ten years, this incident would either be completely irrelevant because our friendship didn't last and I had forgotten about him, or we'd still be in touch and I'd have a ten-year pal on my side so it would be critical. So trying to talk it out again would either be pointless in ten years, or it would pay off handsomely.

It only took me two minutes to realize that I needed to speak with him again.

I made a far more thoughtful and long-term decision.

How Does This Apply to You

Your brain is built to seek immediate gratification. Looking at long-term gratifications and their consequences, on the other hand, permits you to make more informed decisions.

> *Happiness might be described as the fruit of the desire and ability to sacrifice what we want now for what we want later.*

This strategy encourages you to think harder, think smarter, judge the scenario based on both long and short-term perspective and prevents you from quick reactions that could have adverse long-term consequences.

Uncertainty is the nightmare of any decision-maker. It translates to lots of *what-ifs* and leads to endless debate, paralysis by analysis, and confusion, which further magnifies when you consider the long-term effects of your choice. The further something lies in the future, the more parameters can change and cut down the decision tree you gave so much care.

Let's say you're debating whether or not to quit your job and travel the world for a year or two because you've always dreamt of it. Still, you're indecisive, because *what if things go wrong*?

You're absolutely right to ask that question.

> *But you should also ask yourself what if things go right?*

First, the worst case. You'll miss out on the shekels because you're not working. It might be hard to pick up your career where you left it. You won't see your family and friends for a while. The weather might suck and people will call you dumb. You'll decide everything sucks and come back home after three months. How much of a negative impact will all of this have on your life ten years from now?

Now for the best-case scenario. You're having a great time. For a year or two, you acquire unique memories and experiences, widen your horizons, and thoroughly enjoy your life. You'll always have hilarious stories to tell, stunning images to display, and fantastic experiences to look back on if you learn a little bit of a new language. You return with a new perspective on life, new friends, and perhaps even a new love interest. If all goes well, your cultural understanding, and travel experience will all help you land a job.

Now, after ten years, how much of a positive impact will this have on your life?

Assigning numbers to long-term scenarios is a great way to make sense of the myriad of different possible outcomes.

Better Decisions, Better Life

Making good selections isn't difficult, but it does necessitate a specific mindset. Long-term thinking is required, and you must resist being persuaded by ephemeral emotions and impulses.

If you've been debating a major life issue, now is the moment to reconsider and make a better conclusion. Being in the now may be liberating. However, in order to produce a large number of great experiences, you must make wise judgements and plan ahead.

Chapter 23

Average of 5 People

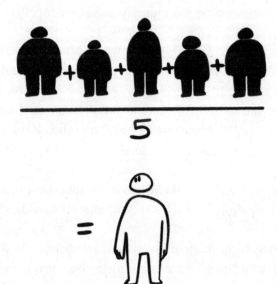

We are the average of five people we spend most of our time with.

You want to be richer, surround yourself with richer people.

You want to be fitter, be around fit people.

You want to be happy, spend time with happy people.

PayPal is a company providing money transfer services that was founded in 1998 In 2002, it was purchased by eBay. The original PayPal employees had difficulty adjusting to eBay's more traditional corporate culture and within four years all but twelve of the first fifty employees had left. They remained connected as business acquaintances. Some of them came to be known as the PayPal Mafia because they went on to found their own companies, some individually and some together.

Entrepreneurs like Elon Musk, Jawed Karim, Reid Hoffman, Premal Shah, Peter Thiel, Jeremy Stoppelman and Russel Simmons are a part of the PayPal Mafia. Elon Musk went on to become the CEO of Tesla and the founder of SpaceX and OpenAI. Jawed Karim co-founded YouTube, Reid Hoffman co-founded LinkedIn, and Premal Shah is the co-founder of Kiva. Peter Thiel is the co-founder of Palantir Technologies and Founders Fund, and the first outside investor of Facebook. Jeremy Stoppelman and Russel Simmons co-founded Yelp.

The fact that all of them retained their acquaintances with each other and went on to be successful in their ventures is not a coincidence. Each of them surrounded themselves with smart and hardworking people. Their company had a major effect on the success of their business ventures. The story of the PayPal Mafia is an example of how useful good company can be. Surround yourself with people you aspire to be like.

If you want to be successful, surround yourself with people who are successful. It will help you gain insights for your own path.

Jim Rohn, an entrepreneur, author, and motivational speaker, said,

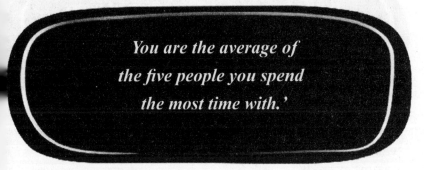

You are the average of the five people you spend the most time with.'

This statement is based on studies that indicate how important our connections are in our lives.

Whether we like it or not, individuals closest to us have a huge influence on our relationships. It has an impact on how we think, how we feel about ourselves, and how we make decisions. If you're reading this book, you're probably interested in continuing your personal development, building effective routines, and reducing the roadblocks between you and your objectives. You understand the need of continuing to grow as a friend, employee, leader, husband, parent, and so on.

Exposing yourself to people who you regard to be successful is an important aspect of preparing for success. If you aren't intentional about who you spend your time with, you won't be able to make the constant personal improvement that you desire. But how often do you find yourself coming to a halt, assessing the crowd, and determining that some changes are necessary? Probably not very often. We underestimate the value of the company we keep.

> ***While having a strong group of peers isn't the main factor in your success, each small step matters!***

While having a strong group of peers isn't the main factor in your success, each small step matters!

So, if you have one toxic friend who tends to drag you down and you tell yourself, 'Well, I only see this person for about an hour a week, so it's not a big deal,' you might want to reconsider. Do you interact more often with this person than with others who are encouraging, motivating, or supportive? If that's the case, Rohn thinks the weekly interaction will be devastating.

Five lessons to learn

1. Keep Your Critics Around

It's easy to believe that the best strategy is to make sure that the five people you spend the most time with are your most ardent supporters. This isn't always the case, though. If you want to be an expert, you'll need someone in your life to provide you with constructive criticism on your work. Constructive criticism helps you to reconsider your strategies (or make new ones) and identify areas of improvement.

2. Consider the Company You Keep Both Online and Offline

It's not surprising that you'd adopt the mindset of the individuals with whom you spend your time because you're exposed to their thoughts and values. Since online communities are quite popular these days, the individuals that you meet online can affect you just as much as your offline company.

You can take advantage of this.

> *Join mastermind groups with people you believe have good ideas. You can gain from their insights and opinions to improve your job.*

It's also a good idea to have an accountability partner on hand, as this will allow you to receive more individualised help.

3. You Can Control the Amount of Time You Spend with People

You have the ability to choose who you spend your time with. The majority of your time is probably spent with your family. While you may not want to completely isolate yourself from family members, you can take a step back to assess whether somebody is bringing you down or has a negative effect on you. If you're being intentional about how you spend your time, you don't have to spend the majority of your time with family just because you're related. Prioritize quality above quantity when spending time with family, friends or colleagues.

4. You Can't Surround Yourself with Negative People and Expect to Have a Positive Life

You may have long-time friends who were a lot of fun when you were younger but who haven't changed or matured since then. As you get older, the people in your life will change, as will your goals and routines. To sustain your social environment, you can't rely on how things have always been in the past.

> *Spending time with people you respect will drive you to act more like them, allowing you to see the value in yourself that you previously overlooked.*

You're more likely to live a happy life if you're surrounded by individuals you respect, rather than being surrounded by people who you are just spending time with because you have known them for a long time.

5. Be One of the Five People to Someone Else

As you grow throughout your life and career and come into contact with people whose shoes you were once in, aim to be one of the five people that they want to spend their time with. Teaching is one of the most effective methods to learn, and placing yourself in a position to do so can benefit both you and your mentee. You must first respect yourself in order to be respected by others. This will give you the confidence you need to achieve and progress through different periods of your life, both personal and professional.

Exercise: Identify your core circle

Let us do an exercise now. Pick up your pen and paper, and then write down your answers to the following questions:

1. *What kind of person do you want to be?*

What is the ideal self you wish to become? What qualities do you wish to possess?

2. *Who are the five people you spend the most time with currently?*

What are they like? What top three qualities do each of them represent?

3. *Do they match who you want to be in the future?*

Do their qualities match who you want to become? Do they help support you or detract you from your vision for yourself? Do they elevate you or bring you down?

4. *Who are the top five people who embody the qualities*

you desire?

They should be people you respect or aspire to become. It can be someone who has already achieved the end state or the goal that you want to achieve. There are no rules here—it does not matter whether the person is a celebrity or a general person, whether he/she is a personal friend or someone outside your social circle, or whether he/she is alive or dead. It can be Oprah, Benjamin Franklin, Albert Einstein, Barack Obama, or whoever you want it to be. Let your imagination run wild!

If one of your job goals is to be a chef, one of the five persons you can name is the Iron Chef or a world-renowned, worldwide award-winning chef. If you want to drop a hundred pounds, make a list of people who have already achieved this goal or who have the body type/weight you desire. If you wish to be a movie producer, think of Steven Spielberg, James Cameron, Christopher Nolan or Peter Jackson as examples of successful producers.

5. How can you increase contact with them?

Depending on who the people are, you can use the following methods to reach out to them:

Direct contact:

This can be face-to-face contact, telephone, or email/internet. How can you increase the opportunities of interacting with this person? If you know the person, how can you communicate with him/her more often? If you don't know the person, does this person belong to a certain community that you can be part of? Do you have any friends who might know this individual? Is there a way for you to join the same social circles?

Products of their work:

If direct communication does not work out, you can always bring the person to you in the form of his/her work. Does the person have any work under his/her name, such as shows, books or podcasts? Get your hands on them and soak yourself in them. These materials were after all made by them and the content will convey their consciousness and knowledge. In essence, being exposed to these materials is the same as interacting with these people.

Visualisation:

This one sounds like the most airy-fairy method out of the three, but it can actually be the most powerful. Clear your mind and visualize these people mentally. Then, mentally consult them and observe their responses to whatever you ask. It can also be used in daily life, where you project their persona in varying life situations and think/act the way you think they will.

Napoleon Hill wrote in Think and Grow Rich that every night before he slept, he would have an imaginary council meeting with his 'invisible counsellors.' The council started out with a group of 9; it eventually expanded to over 50. It included people like Darwin, Einstein, Aristotle, Confucius, and Socrates. Through these nightly council meetings, he received immense inspiration, knowledge, and ideas which he credited for his success in life.

Final Thoughts

So, do you think you are the average of five people?

Are the people you spend the most time with the same people that you admire? If not, you're likely not setting yourself up to be on the road to success.

Think about the people that you spend the most time with. If you lack a sense of pride for their values, ideals or work ethic, it may be time to reconsider their role in your life.

In the age of social media, this principle has evolved; you might be the average of the five content creators whom you consume. It could be the stand-up comedians, or tech reviewers, or even vloggers that you watch.

Chapter 24

Boiling Soup Syndrome

Nobody wants to be in a boiling soup
But growth begins outside one's comfort zone

To bring our mind in an absolute state of alert,
we have to jump in the boiling soup

Walt Disney was widely regarded as a visionary. He found popularity with Mickey Mouse, a biped mouse who could talk. He followed up with *Three Little Pigs*, which was also a big hit in 1933. 'Who's fearful of the Big Bad Wolf?' became an anthem during the Great Depression.

Someone suggested that he should draw more pig-related cartoons since people wanted to see more of them. Disney objected at first, but eventually gave in. The three pig follow-ups, however, were all unsuccessful. Disney realised, 'I couldn't top pigs with pigs., And he started production on his first full-length animated feature film, *Snow White and the Seven Dwarfs*.

Even though Disney was great at what he did, he couldn't grow if he stuck to the same thing. He couldn't make cartoons about pigs all his life and expect all of them to be as well received by the audience as the first one did. After a point, he had to move on to new things and push his limits in order to retain his audience and popularity.

Once you have mastered something, it becomes your comfort zone. But you can't stay within your comfort zone forever.

> *You need to push yourself and seek discomfort if you want to continue growing and being a master.*

Christian Bale is well known not just for his acting but how well he adapts to his characters. He is a master of transformation. From gaining and losing weight, putting on muscles, shaving his head to doing special exercises to thicken his neck, Bale has done everything in his power to stay true to his characters.

He was quite slim, but he followed a strict diet of just lean protein, no sugar, good fats and low carbs for his role in *American Psycho*. In 2004, he stuck to a diet of water, an apple and a cup of coffee per day and lost sixty pounds for his role in *The Machinist*. Right after The Machinist, Bale played the role of Batman for the first time in the 2005 film *Batman Begins*. With just five months to transform, he gained weight by eating pizza and ice cream and sometimes eating five meals at a time. He trained in the gym and lifted weight to sculpt himself while gaining weight.

In 2013, Bale went from being 228 pounds to 285 pounds for his movie *American Hustle*. He ate doughnuts and cheeseburgers and whatever he could get his hands on. He went on to be nominated for the Academy Awards for Best Actor for his role in *American Hustle*.

Bale is a living example of pushing your limits. He does not take up any work half-heartedly. Once he decides on a role, he creates a new benchmark for himself instead of letting the old one restrict him. He always lives outside his comfort zone. This is what distinguishes him from his contemporaries and has made him a great favourite among the audience.

He has however decided not to do any more drastic transformations. Every body has limits, even his, and he has pushed it to its limits.

'Get out of your comfort zone!'

You've heard that statement before; it is now firmly embedded in cultural discourse. But what *is* the comfort zone? And why do we happily stay inside it even if, deep down, we know it mightn't be the best place for us to be?

The ability to take risks by stepping outside your comfort zone is the primary way to grow. But we are often afraid to take that first step.

> *In truth, comfort zones are not*
> *about comfort, they are about fear.*
> *Break the chain of fear to get outside.*

Once you do, you will learn to enjoy the process of taking risks and growing in the process.

What Is the Comfort Zone in Psychology?

The metaphor of 'leaving one's comfort zone' became popular in the 1990s. It was coined by management thinker Judith Bardwick in her 1991 work *Danger in the Comfort Zone*:

'The comfort zone is a behavioural state within which a person operates in an anxiety-neutral condition, using a limited set of behaviours to deliver a steady level of performance, usually without a sense of risk.'

Within the comfort zone, there isn't much incentive for people to reach new heights of performance, causing their progress to plateau. But the concept can be traced further back to the world of behavioural psychology. One of the first investigations that revealed a relationship between anxiety and performance was undertaken by Robert Yerkes and John Dodson in 1907.

When mice were given electric shocks of increasing severity, they grew more driven to complete mazes – but only to a point. They began to hide rather than perform once they passed a certain point.

The same behaviour has been observed in humans. The reasoning behind it is that the alternatives for dealing with anxiety-inducing stimuli are: fight (face the challenge), flight (run away/hide), or freeze (become paralyzed).

The Yerkes–Dodson Law applies to many aspects of life, including knowing ourselves, relating to others, and so on. Our neural systems have a Goldilocks zone of arousal. If you eat too little, you'll stay in your comfort zone and become bored. But if you do it too much, you'll enter the 'panic' zone, which will stymie your progress.

From Comfort Zone to the Growth Zone

Taking a risk and stepping out of your comfort zone demands courage. The new environment and lack of 'comfort' might be a challenge at first, but this is only natural; you needn't panic. Once you stick it out long enough, you enter the learning zone where you pick up new skills and come up with inventive solutions to difficulties.

> *After a time of learning, a new comfort zone emerges, allowing one to reach even greater heights. This is what it means to be in a development zone.*

Moving into the development zone, like other behavioural change attempts, becomes more difficult without some level of self-awareness. Thus, it can be beneficial for readers to consider the following:

The edges of your comfort zones

Everyone's zones vary in size across all life domains. You must understand where the edges of your comfort zone lie in order to breach them. You must also be aware of where your panic zone is located. Taking on challenges that fall somewhere between these zones will push you to grow without overwhelming you.

Know your strengths

Understand and capitalize on your personal strengths. Most people have experienced leaving their comfort zone in at least one area of life, and the experience offers a wealth of insight.

Appreciate the non-linearity

In reality, the process of moving from the comfort zone to a growth zone may be complicated by peaks, troughs, and plateaus. Sometimes we even need to retreat to the comfort zone periodically before mustering the strength to leave again. Accepting this as part of the process can help in tolerating uncertainty.

While occupying the comfort zone, it's tempting to feel safe, in control, and that the environment is on an even keel.

The best sailors, however, aren't born in smooth waters.

To understand what is inside your comfort zone, a simple exercise is to draw a circle on a piece of paper. Everything you are experiencing in your life right now is inside your comfort zone (your circle): your current state of health, your personal fitness, your style of parenting, the friendships you have, your current job, your financial state, and so much more.

Everything you desire but do not currently have in your life is just outside the circle. To get it inside, you're probably going to have to do something new or different. You're going to have to step outside of your comfort zone.

Stepping outside your comfort zone is vital. Here are some of the reasons why.

1 – Personal Growth

A mind once stretched never returns to its original dimension. Just ike ships, humans were not designed to operate within the confines of the safe harbour. We were designed to sail the wide expanses of the oceans and unlock our dormant potential. Growth is one of the six basic human wants, and the only way to achieve it is to be comfortable with discomfort.

2 – Create Momentum

When you start to challenge yourself to step out of your comfort zone, a natural momentum occurs. What can seem like small marginal gains start to stack together; the multiplying effect of the small gains in a number of areas creates a force and rhythm which becomes self-perpetuating. It just cannot be stopped.

3 – *Productivity Ninja*

With increased levels of focus, self-confidence and belief, you start moving toward your vision. You become a productivity ninja, doing things you never thought possible.

4 – *Eliminate Fear*

Your thinking can either help you or hurt you. You have complete and total power over your thoughts. If you don't deliberately program your mind to work for you, it will begin to work against you by default. By trying to keep you from harm, your mind can have a significant impact on your capacity. But once you get started, you'll realise you underestimated your ability.

5 – *The Performance Zone*

You will automatically venture outside your comfort zone and operate in the space I call the performance zone. You learn by stretching and pushing the boundaries, exploring new ideas, failing fast and recovering quickly, discovering what works and bottling it so you can repeat it again. This is the zone where you can get extraordinary outcomes.

6 – *Self-fulfilled*

So many people wake up every day with a painful sense of underachievement...the knowledge that they aren't enjoying their lives to the fullest. Growth, forward momentum, increased productivity and the ability to shape your own performance zone all lead to a sense of self-fulfilment. You'll discover a new source of immense pleasure.

7 – *Profound impact on others*

We all want to be among people we respect and who push us to be the best version of ourselves—people from whom we can learn and who motivate us to leave our comfort zones. By venturing outside your comfort zone, you become a magnet, drawing people into your life who can assist you in your journey toward your goals. Moreover, you become a role model or coach for others, whether consciously or unintentionally.

The Final Word

Remember that you are considerably more capable than you ever anticipated. Your hopes, ambitions, and objectives are all waiting for you. Cultivating a mindset that lays firm foundations and clears the way to the development zone is crucial. This involves believing in your abilities to overcome fears and uncertainty and seeing yourself as naturally adaptable. There are numerous advantages to be achieved throughout one's life if this becomes a habit. We avoid not only disappointments and regrets, but we also reach our full human potential and become role models for others.

'Anything that can go wrong, will go wrong.'

This is a statement made by a renowned British pilot named Murphy, whose adages together formed Murphy's Laws (of which this is one.)

This is an example of a mental model—a belief or framework of how we view the world. This statement vocalises our internal groan when we get out of bed and drop our phones while fumbling about to stop that infernal alarm—stumble to the bathroom and notice the paste tube is empty—mess up our boiled egg—forget our keys—rush to the station only to find the train is leaving. Problems seem to accumulate, one leading to the other like a domino effect.

We might absently toss around this phrase, but the fact is that internalizing this mental model will help us live more consciously. By helping us link together all our ideas of our world, mental models simplify complex thoughts. They improve the quality of our thinking and set frameworks for making decisions. In order to help you build your own framework of models, we've summarized the most relevant ones.

Chapter 25

Second-Order Thinking

Imagine a rock is thrown into a lake.

The splash is the first-order effect. The ripples
are the second-order effects.

The world is filled with first-order thinkers—it's
easy.

Dig deeper.

Always ask "and then what?"—consider the
layers of consequences.

Have you ever taken a decision you thought was failsafe only to find out later that it had unforeseen consequences?

Consider yourself a team leader for a goods manufacturing company. You set an ambitious goal for your team to produce 20% more goods in the following six months to enhance productivity.

Your team ends up creating 30% more as a result of this stretch goal. You say, why, that's fantastic! Is that so?

After the festivities have died down, you notice that things are beginning to fall apart. You learn that the warehouse staff is unprepared to handle the surge, which is causing a backlog. Revenues are down due to an unanticipated decline in customer demand. Your ostensibly smart concept costs your company money.

Your initial decision appeared logical on the surface (and had a positive local effect), but you failed to consider the potential for wider consequences - and this is what 'second-order thinking' is all about.

'Failing to consider second and third-order repercussions is the root of a lot of painfully terrible judgments,' says Ray Dalio, a wealthy American investor and philanthropist. 'It is especially lethal when the initial inferior option confirms your biases. Never take the first available option, no matter how appealing it appears to be, without first asking questions and exploring.' So, let's look at how you may use second-level or second-order thinking to improve your decision-making and accelerate your success.

First-order thinking is concerned with fixing a specific problem with little or no regard for the long-term ramifications. 'First-order thinking is simplistic and shallow, and just about everyone can do it,' Marks says.

As our example above illustrates, most decisions require a deeper level of investigation, which is the essence of second-order thinking.

> *When you look beyond the obvious and immediate, you can make wiser judgments that will give you a higher chance of a positive long-term outcome.*

Although the idea of first-order thinking may appear silly, our minds are wired to seek the simplest solution. We must struggle to see beyond our initial conclusion. This is especially true when we are stressed for time, unskilled in our role or area (or overconfident in our abilities), dealing with powerful emotions, or isolated from other viewpoints.

Our thinking is also affected by our psychological biases and heuristic methods of problem-solving. So, while the concept is straightforward, second-order thinking is a skill that we must develop.

How to use it?

Using second-order thinking can be a purely mental exercise or you can write it down. Consider a decision you have to make. Start by looking at the most immediate effects of making this decision – the first order. Then for each of the effects ask yourself: 'And then what?' That's how you examine the second-order of this decision's consequences. You can repeat this for as many orders as you find practical.

Alternatively, think about the decision in different timelines. Like we discussed earlier, the 10-10-10 rule. Ask yourself:

What will be the consequences of this decision in

Ten minutes?

Ten months?

Ten years?

This way you can think about the short-term, medium-term and long-term consequences of your decision.

You can apply second-order thinking to big decisions (e.g. buying a house), but also small, seemingly mundane, decisions (e.g. eating a cake). It's a very universal tool that is relevant not just in personal life, but also in business or policy-making.

Second-order thinking in practice

Let's explore what second-order thinking looks like in action.

Consider the decision of buying a house outside of the city. The immediate effects might be having a garden, more space for your family, but also suddenly living an hour away from work.

Now look at the higher-order consequences of each:

- *having a garden → able to grow your produce → having fresh herbs and vegetables*

- *more space for family → more rooms to clean → more stress from a messy home*

- *living an hour away from work → need to buy a car → spending two hours of each day in a car*

Obviously, this is just a small subset of consequences for such a big decision, but it shows how second-order thinking can help you see the more long-term consequences. You can now make a more informed and thoughtful decision.

Difference between first-order thinking and second-order thinking

Within-the-box thinking is first-order thinking; it seeks simple solutions based on previous experiences and ideas. It emphasises the immediate impact of our activities while ignoring the long-term consequences. Desiring rapid gratification is an example of first-order thinking at work.

We use this way of thinking when we need to make quick decisions without expending effort, and it is particularly useful in those instances. A large portion of our daily decisions—what to wear to work, where to meet a friend for dinner, which turns to take on the way to work—is governed by first-order thinking. But because of the customary nature of first-order thinking, we are limited to achieving the same outcomes as everyone else.

To summarise, first-order thinking is superficial, reactionary, obvious, quick, and traditional, with an emphasis on the instantaneity of the impact.

Second-order thinking, on the other entails thinking outside the box. By its very definition, it goes beyond our present thoughts and assumptions, painstakingly and carefully uncovering the long-term consequences of our decisions. Given the complexities and uncertainty of our actions, it necessitates intentional and rational thinking.

Great thinkers distinguish themselves from the ordinary by going beyond intuition and pursuing unorthodox solutions using second-order thinking philosophy. They outperform others and achieve higher success.

Second-order thinking is difficult, complex, ambiguous, and unusual; the purpose is to investigate potential future implications and maximise its benefits.

How to develop second-order thinking to make better decisions

To develop second-order thinking skills, we must evaluate the impact of first-order effects by creating a template using these steps:

1. Note down the first solution that comes to your mind with

its immediate positives and negatives. This is your first-order of thinking.

2. Then ask 'What will be the future consequences of this decision?' This evaluates the second and third level consequences (all the way to the nth level). For each decision and level, write its corresponding positives and negatives.

3. Ask questions—the more the better. The purpose of these questions must be to learn:

   • *The risks associated with this decision*

   • *How the decision impacts others*

   • *What others think about the decision*

   • *Why you think you decision is right*

   • *Whether simpler solutions exist*

4. Choose the decision where second and third-order consequences are positive even though the immediate consequences may not be positive. In short, forgo short-term gain in favour of long-term gain.

5. Learn to recognise and apply feedback loops. It may not help with your current decision, but over time it will enable you to make better decisions.

Once you adopt a second-order thinking mental model and start applying its template in your decision process, you will see the positive results of your efforts compound over time.

Examples of second-order thinking

More often than not, our actions have unanticipated and unintended consequences. An practical example might help in understanding how first-order thinking limits and second-order thinking gives way to better decisions .

Example: Managing a work-related crisis

When dealing with a crisis at work, a manager can adopt either first-order or second-order thinking.

First-order thinking: I have done it in the past. I know how to do it way better than anyone else in the team. Let me take over and resolve it for now. My team can learn later.

First-order thinking consequence: The manager will need to intervene every time there's an issue. The team will not be able to solve problems on their own; consequently their development will stagnate, which will result in low team morale.

Second-order thinking: I have done this in the past. I know how to do it way better than anyone else in the team. But if I continue solving it, I will never give an opportunity to my team to step up and resolve issues on their own. This is an excellent opportunity for my team to learn how to manage and deal with crisis situations. I will instead guide them through the process.

Second-order thinking consequence: Although the team might take slightly longer to solve problems, they will actually learn how to do so. The manager can instead plan how to reduce the number of such crisis situations. The team also feels motivated and empowered to do more and better.

In this example, first-order thinking has short-term benefits with long-term negative impacts. Second-order thinking has short-term pain with multiple benefits in the long run.

Which one will you choose as a manager?

A lot of extraordinary things in life are the result of things that are first-order negative, second-order positive. Just because things look like they have no immediate payoff doesn't mean that's the case. All it means is that you'll have less competition if the second and third-order consequences are positive, because everyone who thinks in the first order won't think things through.

Chapter 26

Bull-Shit Asymmetry

Principle

The energy required to refute bullshit is much larger than the energy required to produce it.

This is why Bull-Shit (BS) spreads so easily—especially on social media.

It's also why we need to make a deliberate effort to fight back against it.

The Science of Bullshit

In the world of fake news, bullshit deserves to be studied more properly than ever before. What is bullshit? Why do people bullshit? Why is bullshit so hard to refute?

> *Bullshit is a statement made without regard to the truth and connotes overstatement, exaggeration, or falsehood.*

Spewing bullshit, however, is not the same as lying; rather, the bullshitter has no real knowledge or care as to whether what they are saying is truthful or not. A bullshitter is not constrained by the truth but isn't necessarily lying.

Prof. Frankfurt summarizes:

'The liar asserts something which he himself knows to be false. He deliberately misrepresents what he takes to be the truth. The bullshitter, on the other hand, is not constrained by any consideration of what may or may not be true. In making his assertion, he is indifferent to whether what he is says is true or false. His goal is not to report facts. It is, rather, to shape the beliefs and attitudes of his listeners in a certain way.'

Who is a Bullshitter?

In a fascinating study, researchers at the IZA Institute of Labor Economics in Germany analysed over forty thousand teens in nine Anglophile countries, including the U.S., to determine the characteristics of bullshitters. According to their research, here are the characteristics of people more likely to be bullshitters:

- Men are much more likely to be bullshitters than women

- Bigger bullshitters are more confident than those who bullshit less. Bullshitters are more likely to say they 'can handle a lot of information', 'can easily link facts together', 'are quick to understand things', and 'like to solve complex problems'

- Young people from more advantaged socio-economic backgrounds have higher average bullshit scores than their less advantaged peers

- Immigrants are more likely to bullshit than non-immigrants, but being a non-immigrant was nearly a flat correlation. So being an immigrant is correlated to being a bullshitter, but not being an immigrant doesn't really make you less likely to be one.

- People from the U.S. and Canada are much bigger bullshitters than those in Europe, Australia or New Zealand

Why is bullshit so hard to refute

Bullshit, by its very nature, is often hard to refute. It typically isn't an out-and-out lie, but instead an exaggeration, a statement that is close to the truth or sounds like it should be true. It is easy to spew bullshit and sound correct.

For example, consider the following statement:

'People in Canada are actually in favour of global warming. A warming planet will mean that their property values will increase dramatically as their Arctic climate becomes more temperate.'

This is not true. However, it does sound plausible. Maybe it *is* true. Maybe it's bullshit. Now think about how much research it would take to disprove that statement. I'd have to find surveys on Canadian views of global warming—not just whether they believe it's happening or man-made, but also whether they welcome it. Even if I could find a survey addressing this specific point, it would probably be skewed as it's highly unlikely that anyone would admit to such an opinion. So, my simple bit of bullshit would take quite a bit of effort to refute, whereas thinking of it and typing it out took no time or effort at all.

There's another aspect to bullshit; you've probably experienced it already. Now that you've read the above sentence about Canadians liking global warming, you might be thinking: 'huh, I actually wonder whether Canadians like global warming. It does sound plausible.' Maybe at a party, or hanging out with friends, you might say 'I heard that Canadians are in favour of global warming, what do you think?'

This is how bullshit spreads – it sounds plausible and is repeated. A future report stating that Canadians aren't actually in favour of global warming may not spread as quickly, because a refutation isn't as 'sticky' or 'viral' as the juicy gossip-like bullshit statement that Canadians are in favour of cooking the earth!

Bullshit can be more dangerous than a lie. As noted by professor Frankfurt above, a bullshitter's goal is 'to shape the beliefs and attitudes of his listeners in a certain way.' Bullshit often appeals to our emotions or to our existing worldviews.

> *Once ideas become lodged in our emotions or confirm our views of the world, they can become extremely hard to dislodge – even by the truth.*

Once ideas become lodged in our emotions or confirm our views of the world, they can become extremely hard to dislodge – even by the truth.

The burden of proof should not fall on those who have to refute bullshit. Let's hold bullshitters accountable for their own bullshit! As Annie Duke suggests in her excellent book *Thinking in Bets*, when someone states something, ask them how certain they are of it in terms of how much would they bet that it's true.

While bullshit predates the internet, the internet makes the problem much worse because it is very easy to publish and spread an opinion on the internet.

Have a healthy dose of scepticism about pretty much everything.

Chapter 27

Cobra Effect

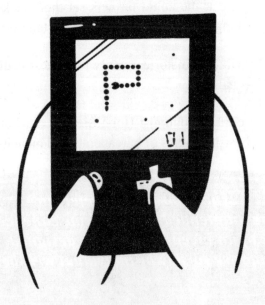

When a measure becomes a target, it ceases to be a good measure.

Fearing the cobras in India, the British offered bounties for cobra heads.

So locals bred cobras to turn in their heads.

A policy designed to reduce the cobra population had the opposite effect.

Many years ago, so the story goes, there was a cobra infestation in Delhi during the colonial era. The British created a bounty for cobra skins in the assumption that the public would capture feral cobras for the reward. Instead, people started farming cobras for their skins. The British eventually got wise to the cobra-farming industry and cancelled the bounty. But with no bounties to collect, the cobra farmers set their snakes free in the city—making the infestation even worse than before.

It's from this (likely ahistorical) story that the so-called Cobra Effect gets its name.

Coined by German economist Horst Siebert, the Cobra Effect can ruin the best-laid plans of bureaucrats and business people.

> *The Cobra Effect refers to the unintended negative consequences of an incentive that was designed to improve society or individual well-being.*

A related term is Perverse Incentives, which refers to incentives that have an unwanted result that does not fulfil the desires of their designers.

We begin to see connections in the world around us as soon as we are born. A meal satisfies hunger; sleep satisfies exhaustion; problems have causes; and removing the cause leads to a solution. Whether we are aware of it or not, we are creating mental models of how cause and effect are related.

Our mental models have a huge influence on how we think and

see things. They determine what we perceive, inform us about significant events, assist us in making sense of our experiences, and give useful cognitive shortcuts to help us think faster.

They can, however, lead us wrong. The majority of our cause-and-effect encounters involve basic, direct links. As a result, we have a tendency to conceive in terms of 'linear' behaviour: double the cause, double the effect; halve the cause, halve the effect. The world is often more intricate than we realise, as we will witness with the Delhi cobras.

Real-World Examples of the Cobra Effect

The 'cobra effect' is a concept that we see all the time in business. Business executives make well-intentioned judgments to solve a problem or achieve a goal. However, if it is not well thought out, it may exacerbate the problem. Firms overpay salespeople for selling products or services that don't benefit their company or customers. As a result, sales agents frequently shift their focus to selling mismatched solutions. This generates a terrible client experience and can be costly to the business.

> *If everyone is simply concerned with short-term gain, they will only exacerbate the problem.*

1. Bogota: Fewer Cars, Less Pollution?

In Bogota, Colombia the government wanted to reduce pollution caused by excess traffic. So, they created a law that only allowed people to drive on certain days of the week, determined by the last two numbers on their license plate.

But lots of families, especially those where both parents worked, needed to drive every day. Instead of buying an illegal license plate and switching it out every day, people solved their issue in a totally legal way: they just bought more cars—sometimes up to four for a single family.

The result? More pollution, and more cars on the road.

2. Wells Fargo: More Accounts, Happier Customers?

American bank Wells Fargo created quotas for the number of new accounts and offered incentives to the employees. But many resorted to secretly opening accounts in customers' names and other unethical practices. This attempt to improve its bottom line resulted in lawsuits, heavy fines, and a terrible PR fiasco.

3. Airbus: Less Noise, Better Flying Experience?

Airplane manufacturer Airbus wanted to improve the flying experience on its planes by reducing noise in its cabins. But once the noise was removed, Airbus realized that the cabin noise was covering up lots of unwanted sounds—like babies crying and toilets flushing. Its attempt to improve flying actually made the experience worse.

4. A Gun Buyback Program Goes Awry

In 2008 the police in Oakland, California conducted a gun buy-back program. Presumably, the goal was to reduce criminals' easy access to firearms. Anyone could turn in a firearm and walk away with $250, no questions asked.

A newspaper account called the buy-back program 'a poorly organized fiasco.'

(This raises the question: What distinguishes a poorly organized fiasco from a well-organized one? I assume that an incompetent fiasco would be worthy of contempt, whereas a skilfully managed fiasco would merit grudging respect. But that is an ontological question beyond the scope of this post.)

So what went wrong here?

The first two people in line at one of the three buyback locations were gun dealers with sixty firearms packed in the trunk of their cars. They bought a dozen guns from seniors living in an assisted-living facility.

Rather than getting guns off the streets, some less-than-trustworthy individuals were turning in their cheap weapons and using the $250 bounty to buy a better gun.

So many people rushed to turn in guns that the police department ran out of money and had to give IOUs, leaving the department with a $170,000 debt.

How to Avoid the Cobra Effect

If you work in marketing, business, or design, you're likely to run across the Cobra Effect. To avoid it, here's economist Steven Levitt's advice:

Create simple incentives. The more complicated you make a scheme, the easier it is to find loopholes.

Try to outsmart yourself. Before you put a reward scheme in place, try and figure out a way to game it, then adjust your program accordingly.

You may not be able to avoid Perverse Incentives completely, but being aware is the first step to avoiding them.

The Lesson

None of this negates the need for law. It does, however, imply that policymakers should be acutely conscious of the fact that every human action has both intentional and unforeseen repercussions. Human beings react to every rule, regulation, and order imposed by governments; and their reactions might produce consequences that are entirely different from those intended by lawmakers. While law has its place, it should be defined by extreme prudence and humility. Unfortunately, these are characteristics that are rarely seen among lawmakers, which is why examples of the cobra dilemma are so common.

While the Cobra Effect is now obvious, it is not always obvious at the outset of a well-intentioned policy that the outcome may be worse. When it comes to human behaviour, it's a good idea to start by asking,

'What might possibly go wrong?'

Chapter 28
First Principle

It's hard to see beyond our world view.

Start with the absolute basics and work backwards.

This is what enables original thinking.

Elon Musk, who is 46 years old, has invented and established three multibillion-dollar firms in very unrelated fields: Paypal (financial services), Tesla Motors (automotive), and SpaceX (space exploration) (Aerospace). Solar City (Energy), which he helped establish and recently acquired for $2.6 billion, isn't even on this list.

At first appearance, his fast success, ability to tackle seemingly impossible challenges, and genius-level creativity appear to be linked to his remarkable work ethic. Musk has indicated that he has worked an average of a hundred hours per week for the past fifteen years and has lately reduced his hours to eighty-five. According to rumours, he doesn't even take lunch breaks, and instead multitasks between eating, meetings, and replying to emails.

There's no denying that work ethic is crucial in unlocking your inner creative genius and being the best at what you do, but there's also the fact that there are highly hard-working people who make little progress in life and die before sharing their best work with the world.

So, what's the missing link between innovative innovation and rapid success?

Aristotle, Euclid, Thomas Edison, Feynman, and Nikola Tesla, among the most brilliant minds of all time, used this missing connection for rapid learning, overcoming challenging issues, and creating outstanding work throughout their lifetimes, much like Musk.

This missing link has
nothing to do with their efforts.
It all comes down to the way they think.

First Principle Thinking

During a one-on-one interview with TED Curator, Chris Anderson, Musk reveals this missing link which he attributes to his genius level creativity and success. It's called reasoning from 'First Principles'.

'Well, I do think there's a good framework for thinking. It is physics. You know, the sort of first principles reasoning. Generally I think there are — what I mean by that is, boil things down to their fundamental truths and reason up from there, as opposed to reasoning by analogy.'

Analogical reasoning is what we typically practice in our daily lives, by essentially copying what other people do with slight variations. We build knowledge and solve problems based on prior assumptions, beliefs and widely held 'best practices' approved by the majority of people.

The polar opposite method of thinking is what Musk referred as first principles thinking.

> *It is the practice of actively questioning every assumption you think you know about a given problem or scenario, and creating new knowledge and solutions from scratch.*

First-principles thinking is one of the best ways to reverse-engineer complicated problems and unleash creative possibilities. Sometimes called 'reasoning from first principles,' the idea is to break down complicated problems into basic elements and then reassemble them from the ground up. It's one of the best ways to learn to think for yourself, unlock your creative potential, and move from linear to non-linear results.

This approach was used by the philosopher Aristotle. It allowed him to cut through the fog of shoddy reasoning and inadequate analogies to see opportunities that his contemporaries missed.

Here are three simple everyday examples of how this works.

Assumption: 'Growing my business will cost too much money.'

First principles thinking:

What do you need to grow a profitable business? I need to sell products or services to more customers.

Does it have to cost a lot of money to sell to new customers? Not necessarily, but I'll probably need access to these new customers inexpensively.

Who has this access and how can you create a win-win deal? I guess I could partner with other businesses that serve the same customer and split the profits 50:50. Interesting.

Assumption: 'I just can't find enough time to work out and achieve my weight loss goals.'

First principles thinking:

What do you really need to reach your weight loss goal? I need to exercise more, preferably 5 days a week for an hour each time.

Could you still lose weight exercising less frequently, and if so, how? Possibly, I could try 15-minute workouts, 3 days a week. These could be quick high intensity full body workouts that will speed up my fat loss in less time.

Assumption: 'I have to struggle and starve to become a successful artist.'

First principles thinking:

What do you really need to create great work and make a good living as an artist? I would need a reasonably sized audience that will appreciate and buy my artwork.

What do you need to reach a larger audience? I probably need to do some marketing, but I don't like self-promoting so I'd rather not do this.

Is there any way for you to promote your work without being sleazy? Yes, if the focus of selling my artwork is meaningful with a purpose of serving the audience — then I could make more money to make more art, so I can serve more people.

Traditional	First Principles
How we typically think	How we should think
Starts with limitations	Starts with the possibilities
Iteration and improvement of an existing path	Define and explore a completely new path
Explore available solutions in the form of variations of what exists without true knowledge	Create a new recipe from the fundamental truth
Look back in time and then determine what to build	Look into the future and its needs
Question the path taken to reach a certain goal	Ask the question 'What's the goal?'

Applying First Principle thinking changes your outlook towards opportunities and goals. In order to apply First Principle thinking, look around and make some counterintuitive observations. Reflect on your first thoughts and whether they are really true.

When you think differently, you don't just change your thoughts but your life.

Chapter 29

Fundamental Attribution

Error

Humans tend to:

(1) Attribute someone else's actions to their character—and not to their situation or context.

(2) Attribute our actions to our situation and context —and not to our character.

We cut ourselves a break, but hold others accountable.

What does it mean?

The basic attribution fallacy is defined as a person's inclination to attribute another's behaviour to their character or personality rather than on external environmental causes beyond their control. To put it another way, you hold others completely responsible for their behaviour.

The fundamental attribution error is caused by how people view the world. While you have some notion of your own character, goals, and circumstances, you rarely have a complete picture of what's going on with someone else.

It's easy to see how the fundamental attribution error (FAE) might affect your personal life, but it's also crucial to understand how it can affect your professional life.

Cognitive biases such as the FAE can influence how you interact with co-workers and make business decisions.

When you're working with co-workers, for example, you're likely to acquire a rough sense of their personality based on bits and pieces of a situation, but you'll never see the complete picture. While it would be wonderful to give someone the benefit of the doubt, your brain is wired to make decisions based on limited information. Within organisations, FAE can result in everything from squabbles to firings and a schism in the culture. In fact, any misunderstanding in which human motivations can be misconstrued is caused by the FAE.

Fundamental Attribution Error Examples

Example #1: The Late Employee

Susan has an interview with Company ABC at 1 PM. When she gets off the train, she gets pushed by another passenger. Susan sprains her ankle and hops along to the interview as best as she can .

When she arrives, she is over fifteen minutes late. The interviewees tell each other, 'She's not very punctual. It must be something in her character.' 'I don't know if we can trust her to come to work every day on time.'

Despite doing well in the interview, Susan doesn't get the job. The interviewees blame the poor punctuality on her character. Perhaps she is just a disorganised person, but that is not a desirable trait in an employee. Yet the real reason was a situation she could not have foreseen. In turn, there is a fundamental attribution error.

Example #2: The Actor vs the Character

Actors and actresses who play a character on the screen can often be confused with their on-screen characters. For instance, Jennifer Aniston may be seen to have the same characteristics as Rachel from *Friends*.

This can lead to a fundamental attribution error. We may consider Jennifer Aniston and Rachel as one of the same. Her actions may replicate what Rachel would do. However, they are not the same. Jennifer Aniston is merely portraying Rachel; those characteristics are part of acting and are limited to that situation.

Many actors and actresses face such issues in real life. We may expect an actor or actress who portrays an evil villain to be evil and devious in real life. However, we are attributing that to the actor or actress's situation by which they are performing, not their dispositional attributes.

Example #3

Let's say your friend Jake takes you to a party. He introduces you to his other friend Aaron, who seems disinterested and unwilling to talk to you, and generally unpleasant to be around.

It would be fair to conclude that Aaron is simply not a nice person. You may not see why he is friends with Jake in the first place. 'Why are you friends with this guy?' you might say.

On the surface, it may seem like Aaron isn't a nice person. However, what we haven't seen is the fact that his mother passed away last week and he had just been fired from his job.

What we see is a fundamental attribution error. We may assign his bad behaviour towards his personality, or, dispositional attributes. Yet his behaviour is better explained by his situation instead.

Why it Happens

University students read articles that either backed or condemned Fidel Castro, the leader of the Communist Party of Cuba, in a classic study by Edward Jones and Victor Harris. Some participants were informed that the writer had decided whether to write for or against Castro, while others were informed that the writer had been assigned a position.

The researchers were shocked to discover that even when participants were informed that the author had not picked which side to support, they still believed the author's views on Castro were compatible with the arguments they presented in the essay. Similar research has found that this impact occurs regardless of the individuals' own viewpoints. It appears even when they are provided further information on the writer or are warned about bias.

So, why do people commit the FAE despite the fact that they should be aware of situational factors? There are a number of possible causes for this.

Accounting for the situation takes up mental resources

In some cases, the FAE seems to happen in part because it takes effort to adjust our perception of somebody's behaviour to be more in line with the situation they're in. We have limited cognitive resources, and our brains like to take the route that expends as little energy as possible. This leads us to take cognitive shortcuts (known as heuristics), and also makes us vulnerable to a whole raft of cognitive biases.

When we mentally process somebody else's actions, there are three steps we need to go through.

1. *First, we categorize the behaviour. (What is this person doing?)*

2. *Second, we make a dispositional characterisation. (What does this behaviour imply about this person's personality?)*

3. *Finally, we apply a situational correction. (What aspects of the situation might have contributed to this behaviour?)*

While the first two steps seem to happen automatically, the third step requires a deliberate effort—which means it often gets skipped over, especially in situations where we don't have the cognitive resources to go through it. For example, this could happen if we're distracted by something else or if we don't have the time for it.

The FAE is affected by our mood

Research has shown that we are more likely to commit the FAE when we're in a good mood, compared to when we're in a bad mood. In a study based on Jones & Harris' Castro experiment, participants read essays that were for/against nuclear testing, and then made judgments about the writer's opinions on the subject.

However, this study had an added twist. Before reading the essays, the participants completed a verbal abilities test, where they had to complete sentences such as 'Car is to road as train is to...' The questions ranged from easy to hard, including several that didn't actually have any one 'correct' answer (such as 'Bread is to butter as the river is to...').

To manipulate participants' moods, once they finished the test, an experimenter told them that they'd performed either above or below average. They went on to read the essays, with some being told that the writer had picked their argument and others told that they had been forced to argue a specific side.

The results of this study showed that happy participants were more likely to commit the FAE, but only when the writer had been assigned an opinion *and* argued for an unpopular stance.

Overall, it seems like being in a bad mood can make us more vigilant and systematic in our processing, which helps us to pay closer attention and retain more information. In fact, compared to participants who were put in a bad mood, happy participants were able to recall fewer details about the essay they had just read, suggesting that good moods can actually impair memory.

The fact that participants were more prone to the FAE only when they had read an essay with an unpopular opinion might also indicate that they were relying on heuristics (stereotypes) about the people who hold that opinion, and that their happy mood made them less likely to question their reliance on those stereotypes.

To sum up,

Sometimes we ignore the situation on purpose

We've seen that if we don't have enough cognitive resources or something else is interfering with our processing, we may skip the situational adjustment phase and commit the FAE. However, even when we have the cognitive ability to consider things through, we may choose not to. This happens when we believe a behaviour is highly *diagnostic* (indicative) of a specific personality feature.

Let's look at some examples of immoral behaviour, such as stealing or harming another person. People tend to conceive of immoral behaviour as highly diagnostic of immoral psychological qualities, according to studies. In other words, people believe that in order for someone to do anything immoral, they must be an immoral person. They don't always apply the same rationale to moral behaviour—for example, someone who takes an old lady's pocketbook is thought to be bad, but someone who assists an old lady across the street isn't always a saint.

When we analyse highly diagnostic behaviours, we believe that they are both essential and sufficient for us to form judgments about the individual who is engaging in them.

How to Avoid the
Fundamental Attribution Error

Consider the last time you felt a that co-worker or customer care professional deserved to be fired. How frequently have you truly attempted to comprehend the contextual circumstances that may be influencing this person's work? Not very frequently, probably.

> *Gratitude is one technique that can aid in the fight against FAE.*

Because the fundamental attribution error is founded in psychology, conquering it can be challenging. When you're resentful of someone for displaying a negative 'quality,' attempt to think of five positive traits that the person possesses. This can help to balance your viewpoint and allow you to see your co-worker as a full person rather than through the prism of a particular flaw.

It is impossible to entirely overcome FAE; however, you can be kinder and more sympathetic with your co-workers using a combination of mindfulness and a few minor tools and methods.

Another option is to work on improving your emotional intelligence. Over the last two or three decades, this term has become a buzzword in the business world.

> *Emotional intelligence entails practising self-awareness, self-regulation, and other means of becoming more objective in the service of one's long-term goals and the interests of others.*

Empathy training, such as having chats with co-workers about their perspectives on projects and their lives outside of work, is a wonderful beginning step.

Systemic Effects

We are particularly likely to commit the FAE when considering certain kinds of behaviour, including behaviour we consider to be immoral. This can become a barrier to addressing systemic issues in our society.

The FAE vs. the actor-observer bias

The FAE is often confused with a similar phenomenon, the actor-observer bias (also known as actor-observer asymmetry). According to this cognitive bias, people have a tendency to make dispositional attributions for other people's behaviour and situational attributions for their own. In other words, while we like to explain our own actions in terms of the various external factors that might have caused us to act the way that we did when it comes to other people, we are quick to say that they act the way they do because that's just the 'way they are.' The FAE is strictly focused on other people's behaviour while the actor-observer bias focuses on ours as well.

The FAE vs. the Correspondence Bias

The correspondence bias is another bias that is frequently mistaken with the FAE. In fact, the two names were used interchangeably for a long time before scholars began to argue that they were distinct.

The correspondence bias is a psychological phenomenon that describes people's inclination to infer things about other people's personalities based on their actions. To put it another way, we believe that people's actions reflect their innermost feelings. The FAE, on the other hand, discusses how we undervalue the importance of contextual elements.

Although these biases are distinct, the FAE can influence the correspondence bias. Consider the following scenario: you're watching a classmate squirming and stuttering while making a presentation. The FAE may lead you to minimise how difficult the circumstance (making a class presentation) is for most people. As a result of the correspondence bias, you may conclude from your classmate's conduct that they are worried in general.

Chapter 30

The Peter Principle

Employees in hierarchies are steadily promoted for competence—until they reach a level where they're incompetent.

People are promoted up to the level of peak *incompetence*.

Devised as satire, it may explain a lot about senior management at large organizations.

What does it mean?

According to the Peter Principle,

> *Persons who succeed in large hierarchical organisations are promoted until they achieve their level of ineptitude.*
> *They are rarely promoted after that and are often stuck there for the rest of their lives.*

Let's look at an example from real life to better grasp this:

John and Jenny, two graduates, originally met at a sales training for G Pharma reps. They were ecstatic to have landed a job where they could genuinely assist others. GermiEnd, a promising new analgesic, had just been developed by the corporation.

Both were successful in persuading doctors to administer GermiEnd whenever a patient was in agony. They became friends over time and frequently celebrated their accomplishments together. Both had excellent sales results and were eventually promoted to management positions. Jenny was a wonderful salesperson but she lacked management skills, and the shift happened without much training. Jenny's co-workers began to treat her badly, and she got dissatisfied at work. As a result, she decided to put in less effort and became incompetent.

On the other hand, John was a natural at what he did. He knew how to deal with his worst representatives and how to congratulate those who did well. He rose through the ranks of the company, and after a few years, he was promoted to Sales Director.

John's new role as a director was challenging. He lacked the analytical skills required to comprehend statistics. He began working longer hours to compensate for this, but instead of increasing his performance, this just frustrated him further and his competence decreased.

At this point, Jenny started avoiding John whenever she saw him in the cafeteria. She was terrified of revealing her flaws. She became too preoccupied with herself to see how tense he appeared. They lost not only their will to work but also a friendship—all because of a mismatched promotion.

How does Peter's Principle work?

People advance in their careers because they have high skills in a specific task, but these skills might be irrelevant to the new role. The skills they now require are either above their ability level or they may not have received the required training. Their new manager might also be a victim of the Peter Principle and doesn't realise that training would be a good idea.

Then there are incentives at play. People often work hard to reach a certain position or salary, and once they achieve that, most people turn lazy. Once people lose their passion, they stop learning. They may fail to keep up with new developments which leads to poor quality of work. In order to protect their comfort zone, they challenge any new idea or person that can make their lives uncomfortable.

Incompetent employees are often unhappy. They leave a job at which they excelled and earned the respect of their colleagues, and then watch their colleagues get promoted or remain equally stuck. This has a negative impact on the company.

> *Incompetent managers will fear losing their jobs; they will celebrate obscurity and implement complicated procedures, leaving colleagues feeling confused and uninformed.*

Some may work very hard to make up for the lack of skills. For this reason, their supervisors won't dare to let them go.

The end result is a messy and complex situation.

Why do incompetent people think they're amazing

Knowing how competent we are and how our skills stack up against each other is more than a self-esteem boost. It helps us figure out when we can forge ahead on our own decisions and instincts, and when we need to seek out advice.

> *But psychological research suggests that we're not very good at evaluating ourselves. In fact, we frequently overestimate our abilities.*

Researchers have a name for this phenomenon: the *Dunning-Kruger* effect, after the psychologists who studied the phenomenon. This effect explains why more than a hundred studies have shown that people display illusory superiority. We judge ourselves as better than others to a degree that violates the laws of mathematics.

When software engineers at two companies were asked to rate their performance, they put themselves in the top 5%. In another study, 88% of American drivers described themselves as having above-average driving skills.

These aren't isolated findings. On average, people tend to rate themselves better than most in disciplines ranging from health, leadership skills, ethics, and beyond. What's particularly interesting is that those with the least ability are often the most likely to overrate their skills to the greatest extent.

People measurably poor at logical reasoning, grammar, financial knowledge, mathematics, emotional intelligence, and chess tend to rate their expertise almost as favourably as actual experts do.

So who's most vulnerable to this delusion? Sadly, all of us, because we have pockets of incompetence that we don't recognise.

Why does this happen?

Psychologists Dunning and Kruger claimed that people who lack knowledge and aptitude in specific areas suffer from a twofold curse.

> *First, they make errors and make poor decisions. Second, those same knowledge gaps keep them from noticing their own mistakes.*

Poor performers, in other words, lack the skill required to recognise how awful they are performing. The worst 25% of teams in the preliminary rounds of a collegiate debate competition, for example, lost roughly four out of every five matches, according to the researchers. However, they believed they were winning about 60% of the time. The students couldn't tell when or how often their arguments broke down since they didn't understand the rules of debate.

The Dunning-Kruger effect isn't caused by our ego's blindness to our flaws. When people recognise their flaws, they are more likely to admit them. In one study, students who had performed poorly on a logic quiz and then completed a mini-course on logic were more than willing to classify their previous performances as bad.

That could explain why persons with a modest level of knowledge or expertise have a lower level of confidence in their abilities. They've learned enough to realise there's still a lot they don't know. Experts, on the other hand, are usually well aware of their own expertise. However, they frequently make a different error; they think that everyone else is also knowledgeable.

As a result, people, whether inept or skilled, are frequently trapped in a bubble of erroneous self-perception. They can't notice their own flaws when they're untrained, and they don't realise how rare their abilities are until they're highly competent.

What can you do to find out how good you are at certain activities if the Dunning-Kruger effect is undetectable to those who are experiencing it?

First, seek out and evaluate input from others, even if it's difficult to hear.

Second, and most importantly, continue to learn. The more knowledge we gain, the less likely we are to have unseen flaws in our abilities. Maybe it all comes down to the old adage: Before you argue with a fool, be sure the other person isn't doing the same thing.

To sum it up

Dr. Peter summarised the Peter Principle by noting that 'the cream rises till it sours,' a spin on the ancient adage that 'the cream rises to the top.' To put it another way, good employee performance is inevitably promoted to the point where it is no longer excellent, or even satisfactory.

According to the Peter Principle, competence is rewarded with a promotion since competence is visible and hence recognised. When an employee reaches a point where they are inept, however, they are no longer judged on their output, but rather on input characteristics such as coming on time and having a positive attitude.

Dr. Peter went on to say that employees who are incompetent in their jobs prefer to stay in them, since incompetence is rarely enough to get them fired. In most cases, only extreme ineptitude results in dismissal.

Section 6 – Mindset

Deam Kamen has spent his entire life inventing. He's worn a denim shirt, jeans, and work boots and designed everything from medicine infusion pumps to stair-climbing wheelchairs to portable dialysis devices, all of which have been huge triumphs.

Deam built a contraption in the early 2000s that he hoped could eliminate walking and help people navigate around congested cities. All one had to do was stand on it and it would transport them wherever they wanted to go. Segway became the brand name for the product. When Steve Jobs tried it, he refused to get off, believing it to be as revolutionary as the personal computer. He was known for placing large bets based on intuition, and he was persuaded that this was a significant product.

Despite this, the Segway has yet to gain traction as a product, despite the fact that it has been on the market for years. There are a million reasons why it didn't work, and each one is valid. Some believe that, despite the fact that the product has been on the market for several years, it has not yet lost the war. It still has a chance to take off.

This isn't going to stop Deam Kamen from pursuing his dream of inventing stuff for the rest of his life. He continues to play with technology, trying to come up with the next great idea, despite having more than 440 patents to his name. He sincerely feels he can make a difference in the world and continues to work toward that goal.

It is thoughts like these that have the potential to change the world one step at a time. While many people dream of making a difference in the world, few have the necessary mindset.

You're probably expecting me to tell you to be fearless, but that's not the case. Being brave and fearless are sometimes confused, but they are not the same thing. Bravery is enticing. Fearlessness is both frightening and foolish.

> *To make room for ideas,*
> *one must first make room for the abstract.*
> *And, in order to make room for the abstract,*
> *one must also make room for fear.*

In my life, I believe I've made a conscious decision to do so.

Fear and creativity are fraternal twins; how we deal with fear has a direct impact on how we deal with ideas. This is why we must exercise caution.

Every worthwhile endeavour is accompanied by a shit sandwich. And it is our passion for the goal that makes the shit sandwich worthwhile as a reward. It's all too easy to get bogged down and succumb to fear, or, worse, to entirely eradicate it. But the right strategy is to make space for it in a healthy way—it must be present but not overpowering.

When I say fear, I'm not talking about ideophobia. I'm talking about the kind of fear which stops us from trying something because we know we would be bad at it in the beginning. This is the fear we need to manage, not kill.

One of the main goals of this book is to assist the reader in identifying his or her own creative process and forming habits that will help him better grasp how creativity works. We will look at a number of case examples from academic study and situations related to creativity. Knowing what is being studied throughout the world should help one better comprehend what is going on in his or her own brain.

'We are what we repeatedly do,' Aristotle stated. 'Then excellence is a habit, not an act.'

This also refers to living a life of pursuit of ideas. Living an idea-rich life is not an act, but a lifestyle. The goal of this part is to assist you in managing your thoughts so that you can develop an idea mindset.

Chapter 31

Hedonic Treadmill

Humans have a tendency to quickly return to a baseline level of happiness after positive or negative events.

We believe that "more" will make us happier. It won't.

We get there, feel a moment of happiness, and reset to thinking about the next "more" ahead.

Will winning the lottery make you happier?

Imagine winning a multi-million-dollar lottery tomorrow. If you're like many of us, you'd be ecstatic. But would that joy still be present a few years later? Maybe not.

A famous study of twenty-two lottery winners showed that months after winning, their average reported levels of happiness had increased no more than that of a control group who hadn't won the lottery. Some were actually unhappier than they had been before winning. Later studies have confirmed that our emotional well-being, how often and how intensely we feel things like joy, sorrow, anxiety, or anger, don't seem to improve with wealth or status beyond a certain point.

This has to do with a phenomenon known as hedonic adaptation or the hedonic treadmill. It describes our tendency to adapt to new situations to maintain a stable emotional equilibrium.

> *When it comes to feeling happy, most of us seem to have a base level that stays more or less constant throughout our existence.*

Of course, the novelty of better food, superior vacations, and more beautiful homes can at first make you feel like you're walking on air, but as you get used to those things, you revert to your default emotional state.

That might sound pretty gloomy, but hedonic adaptation makes us less emotionally sensitive to any kind of change, including negative ones.

What could it look like

1. Lottery winners

People who win the coveted lottery prize experience high levels of happiness at the time. However, according to psychologists, the winners tend to return to their previous levels of happiness once the novelty of the winning experience wears off.

Some even end up less happy because of the changes in relationships and emotions that would've taken place after the win. The influx of happiness can last about a year but will recede gradually to the normal sense of happiness and well-being.

2. Major accident victims

The study with the lottery winners also looked at people who had suffered an accident that left them paralysed. When asked several months after their accidents how happy they were, they reported levels of happiness approaching their original baseline. So, while the hedonic treadmill may inhibit our enjoyment of positive changes, it seems to also enable our resilience in recovering from adversity.

3. Food

The first bite of delicious food brings about an influx of joy and is deemed to be more pleasurable than the successive bites that come after that. However, after the mood lifts and the ecstatic feeling kicks in, the food treat ceases to bring the influx of joy.

Why lotteries don't make us happier

If you are one of those who think winning a lottery is all you need to live a better and happy life, you might want to consider these factors:

1. *It can be difficult to manage large sums of money, and some lottery winners wind up spending or losing it all quickly.*

2. *It can also be socially isolating. Some winners experience a deluge of unwelcome requests for money, so they wind up cutting themselves off from others.*

3. *Wealth may actually make us meaner. In one study, participants played a rigged game of monopoly where the experimenters made some players rich quickly. The wealthy players started patronising the poorer players and hogging the snacks they were meant to share.*

Let's say a million dollars falls into your lap tomorrow. What do you do with it?

Stop running on this treadmill

Worry not, there are a few ways you can beat this treadmill.

- Spend it on experiences: Findings show that we adapt to extrinsic and material things like a new car or a bigger house much faster than we do to novel experiences like visiting a new place or learning a new skill. By that reasoning, the more you spend money on experiences rather than things, the happier you'd be.

- Spend it on other people: In one study, participants were given some money and were either asked to spend it on themselves or on someone else. Later that evening, researchers called up these participants and asked them how happy they were. The happiness levels of those who had spent the money on others were significantly greater than that of those who had spent it on themselves. And that seems to be true around the world. Another study examined the generosity of over 200,000 people from 136 countries. In over 90% of these countries, people who donated tended to be happier than those who didn't.

- Develop an attitude of gratitude: Gratitude promotes happiness. Practising gratitude is a small and sustainable habit to help you find value in everything you are. You can educate yourself to become more grateful with a gratitude exercise. Every night, write down a few things you feel thankful for. Bad days and frustrating moments are inevitable. Yet, life is still full of moments to be cherished.

> *Take your nightly exercise as an instant to embrace the good in your life. This positive thinking has a cumulative effect that will make you realise what is truly important.*

- Practice daily mindfulness: Mindfulness allows you to live in the moment and appreciate the small things around you that would otherwise go unnoticed. Engaging in daily mindfulness can help you relax and change the way you feel about your experiences, especially the stressful ones. Taking a mind-body-based approach means you'll become more balanced in harmony with a relatively stable level of happiness without ups and downs.

And an exception

It is possible that the hedonic treadmill doesn't apply to all kinds of pleasures. The pleasure received from having plastic surgery appears to be particularly resistant to hedonic adaptation. Multiple studies have found that the vast majority of plastic surgery patients are pleased with their results, and that this satisfaction lasts for a long time.

In a 2013 study, for example, the happiness levels of 544 patients were compared to the happiness levels of 264 people who had contemplated but opted against plastic surgery. Those who had surgery had higher self-esteem and reported higher levels of happiness at three, six, and 12-month check-ins.

Although it is unknown why plastic surgery might defy the hedonic treadmill theory, it does demonstrate that the idea does not apply to all types of experiences. It's possible that 'self-improvement' events, such as plastic surgery, make someone joyful for an extended period of time. Maslow's pyramid, which implies that the highest level of happiness is self-growth, lends some credence to this notion.

The meaning

According to the hedonic treadmill theory, achieving our goals just results in a shift in baseline happiness, making our new level of happiness feel neutral. We need to rethink how we think about and pursue happiness; rather than focusing on our desires, we should concentrate on the things we are pleased we don't have.

Despite the fact that the hedonic treadmill appears to be a feature of life, we are not bound to never be happy. According to research conducted by positive psychologist Sonja Lyubomirsky, living circumstances account for 10% of our happiness, which aligns with the hedonic adaptation theory; but we have influence over 40% of our happiness. As a result,

We must devise techniques to counteract or supplement the hedonic treadmill.

Chapter 32
The Inside-Outside View

We have a natural tendency to favour the inside view—our own independent solution to a problem that incorporates all of our hidden biases.

To make better decisions, we should favour the outside view—one that incorporates the best available data.

The movie *Moneyball* based on Michael Lewis' book tells a real-life story of a professional baseball team and its innovative approach to player valuation. The Oakland A's was a low-budget team forced to play against teams with significantly greater resources. The manager (played by Brad Pitt in the movie) decided to adopt a revolutionary strategy: to pick players based on their performance statistics.

The whole professional baseball market turned out to be valuing players incorrectly. Until then, player valuation relied solely on scouts' judgment. The main problem was that the scout's judgment turned out to be heavily influenced by human bias.

Here are some of the most common biases:

- *Attractiveness Bias: The tendency to evaluate physically attractive subjects more favourably.*

- *'Similar to Me' Bias: The tendency to evaluate subjects that remind people of themselves more favourably.*

- *Anchoring Bias: The tendency to use a given focal point as a reference for further evaluation. E.g. Suppose you have two candidates with equal skill levels, one being tall and another being short. If they are evaluated first on height and then on skill, the taller individual is likely to get a higher skills assessment.*

- *Confirmation Bias: The tendency to make near-instant impressions about people and then try to confirm it with all new data collected.*

In the baseball players' market, the effect of human bias was so

> *If one of the most popular markets in the world could be so poorly understood by experts, could this be affecting other markets in the same way?*

strong that simple statistical measures turned out to be better predictors of success. This insight raises the question:

We typically make decisions by focusing on a specific task and by using information that is close at hand. In turn, we make predictions based on that same narrow and unique set of inputs. The 'inside view' includes anecdotal evidence and erroneous perceptions.

We make the mistake of thinking we are representative of everyone else—but why? It all comes down to three illusions.

- *Illusion of superiority. For example, a heavy majority of us believe we are above-average car drivers, even though that is statistically impossible. Also, it's often the least capable people that show the largest gap between what they think they can do and what they actually can achieve.*

- *Illusion of optimism. Most people tend to believe that their future is bright. You think that the odds of the new restaurant you've launched lasting five years is very high—sadly, new restaurants often fail.*

- *Illusion of control. Think back to the last time you played the game Snakes & Ladders. Players typically throw the dice harder when they need a high number and vice versa for a lower number. People behave as if they have some control over events, even when chance plays a big, if not total, role in the outcome.*

The 'outside view' is different. It asks if there are similar situations that can provide a statistical basis for making a decision.

> *Rather than seeing a problem as unique, the outside view wants to know if others have faced comparable problems and what choices they made.*

The outside view is an unnatural way to think because it forces people to set aside all the cherished information they have gathered.

How to use the outside view to make better decisions

1. ***Sample:*** Gather a large sample of similar situations. Mentors and friends are great resources to get some input for the outside view of your own situation, and larger sample sets are always best.

2. ***Analyse:*** See how things played out in those similar situations, focusing on the decisions made and their resulting effects. Study the distribution of outcomes and note the average and extreme successes and failures.

3. *Adjust:* Make changes to your planning and execution to meet the statistical outcomes, not to meet your own intuitive expectations.

4. *Iterate:* Adjust your planning and execution in the face of new information or evidence. This last concept has taken off in the age of small start-up businesses that 'pivot' to new models in the face of new information.

Understanding the Inside-Outside View Better

Case 1

Beethoven is often regarded as the most gifted musician who has ever lived. He was expected to be a vicious self-critic who could tell which of his works would survive the test of time and which would not. Nonetheless, his personal favourites among his works were not the ones that would be played centuries after his death.

Psychologist Aaron Kozbelt examined Beethoven's letters in which he discussed his feelings about seventy of his compositions and compared them to the opinions of contemporary specialists with centuries of experience with his work. Beethoven was, 33% of the time, incorrect. He had underrated the genius of his work in some cases, while overvaluing it in others. Given that Beethoven had already gotten audience criticism on his work, 33% is a pretty high percentage.

It's difficult to judge what one creates for oneself. It's natural to give it a higher rating than it deserves, and it's a difficult prejudice to overcome. But the reason why Beethoven turned out to be a musical genius was not because of some innate characteristic but because of his hard work. Not being able to produce masterpieces didn't stop him from producing. According to George Alexander Fisher, 'From year to year he kept on in musical composition, feeling his way, not discouraged by his inability to produce anything great.'

Though the outside view might sometimes be harsh, you need to recognise its validity and work towards changing it.

> ***The goal is to match
> the inside and outside views
> for better judgment and performance.***

Case 2

Let's say I secretly tell you a song and ask you to tap out the beat on the table. It may be a well-known hip-hop song or a nursery rhyme, but it should be something that everyone in the room knows. You begin tapping your finger joints on the table and humming the song in your brain while smiling. What are the chances that your audience will be able to figure out what you're tapping?

'They should all be able to guess,' you say. 'It's so self-evident.' This is due to the fact that you are already familiar with the song. You're humming it in your head while you tap it on the table. You can't un-know what you already know, and you can't hear the melody through the ears of someone who hasn't heard it before.

However, according to study, only 2.5% of people can recognise the music, which is exceedingly low. While the individual tapping is blissfully singing the tune in his head, the listeners are hearing a strange succession of taps, possibly in Morse.

Something similar occurs in our daily lives. When we convey what's going on in our heads, we explain only what doesn't seem self-evident to *us*, but we already know what's going on. We end up communicating insufficiently.

People are divided on which group is more likely to succeed: those who express their views insufficiently or those who communicate them sufficiently. However, everyone agrees that only the self-aware succeed in life.

To sum it up

The Inside View is how we view our own situation, relying on our narrow experiences and intuition to make decisions. Our situation is not unique, but we believe it is. We then foolishly ignore the possible similarities to other situations.

The Inside View compels us to contrast our own example with similar situations to make it obviously different somehow. We then over-emphasize those differences, building cognitive dissonance among the situations. Finally, we act out of 'intuition' to ease our brain's discomfort. We think our situation is unique. We have the inside view of why, this time, things are different. We ignore the similarities and statistical outcomes.

The Outside View is how we view other peoples' situations. From the outside, these are common story lines. We can expand the frame of reference and pick up on patterns. We focus on the common threads and common outcomes.

We remove emotion. We make better informed decisions.

Chapter 33
Thoughts Training

Your mindset is a skill

You can train it much like a muscle

And it's the most important change
one can bring

On 31st March, 1973, Muhammad Ali was 5-1 favourite in a boxing match against a virtual unknown, Ken Norton. He was wearing a rhinestone encrusted robe which had 'People's Choice' written on it, gifted to him by Elvis Presley.

Every onlooker was confident that Muhammad Ali was going to devastate his opponent. Ken Norton, however, instead of writing himself off, was thinking on the following line from the poem *Thinking*:

> *Life's battles don't always go*
> *to the stronger or faster man,*
> *but sooner or later the man who wins*
> *is the man who thinks he can*

Norton was reminding himself of what he'd read in the book *Think and Grow Rich*: if you can create what you want in your mind and convince yourself that you're going to do it, you would get it. No matter what it is, you'll achieve your goal.

In the eleventh round, Ken Norton broke Muhammad Ali's jaw and became the North American Boxing Federation Heavyweight Champion. And Ali never wore the robe with 'People's Choice' written on it ever again.

Thoughts themselves may not be tangible, but their effects are. Ken Norton would watch recordings of fights where either he had done well or his opponent had done poorly, to psychologically prepare himself for a fight.

Business students were given two options in an experiment.

The first alternative was to do nothing and sit in the back of the class. They were unable to use their laptops or cell phones. They were told that if they sat like this for five minutes, they would be paid $2.50.

The second choice was to take a seat in the first row and work on word puzzles. When asked how much they expected to be paid for the second option, students stated that they expected to be paid more than $2.50, despite the fact that it appeared to be more enjoyable. The children stated they enjoyed working the puzzles after the five minutes were up, but they still anticipated to be paid more than $2.50.

What factors would you examine while deciding on a career path? Would you want to work as a security guard at a museum if you were paid well ? A guard doesn't have much to do and can barely communicate with people who are always moving. His life is the epitome of a monotonous job. But, does the prospect of making money without having to work hard thrill or frighten you?

Most jobs have a pretty severe component of dullness involved. Athletes must spend hours training; soldiers must spend years pointing their guns at the border; and astronauts must spend a significant amount of time sitting and staring at screens that do not change frequently.

> *A person has a different perspective when choosing a job versus executing it.*

Humans have a tendency to choose jobs with less effort, but what about jobs with fascinating problems?

In the novel *The Martian*, astronaut Mark Watney is stranded on planet Mars and everyone thinks he is dead. His best chance to survive is to establish communication with NASA on earth and save himself till the time he can be brought back.

Adults learn best when presented with a problem they care about. In this case, Mark Watney has the best possible motivation, to learn to survive or to die. This is why he says, 'In the face of overwhelming odds, I'm left with only one option, I'm gonna have to science the shit out of this.'

Mark Watney is not only an astronaut but also a botanist. He uses his knowledge of botany to grow potatoes in his spaceship, using the waste from the toilet as manure, Martian soil as soil and water by burning Hydrogen from rocket fuel (it's okay if you didn't get that). And this is what he said when he was done:

'They say once you grow crops somewhere, you have officially colonized it. So, technically, I colonized Mars. In your face, Neil Armstrong!'

He didn't only solve botany-related challenges but several engineering-related ones as well. To conclude, I'm just going to leave you with this quote from the book:

'At some point, everything's gonna go south on you... everything's going to go south and you're going to say, this is it. This is how I end. Now you can either accept that, or you can get to work. That's all it is. You just begin. You do the math. You solve one problem... and you solve the next one... and then the next. And if you solve enough problems, you get to come home.'

Economist Michael Housman wanted to know why some customer service employees stayed in their positions for years while others quit after only a year. He had access to around thirty thousand employees' data. He predicted, like the rest of us, that individuals with a history of job hopping would leave this job early as well. However, that proved to be false. People who had more than five jobs in the previous five years were just as likely to quit as those who had worked at the same place for five years.

One of the data points obtained by Housman was the internet browser that employees had installed on their computers when they applied for this position. He decided to look into whether there was a link between the browser they used and the amount of time they spent on the work for no apparent reason.

He was startled to learn that employees who submitted their CVs using Firefox and Chrome stayed 15% longer than those who used Internet Explorer or Safari. They were also 19% less likely to be absent from work. Furthermore, they saw a considerable increase in sales, as well as quicker contact times and happier consumers.

Housman hypothesised that it was because Chrome and Firefox users are more tech-savvy, but when tests were conducted and the two groups were compared, it was discovered that both groups were equally skilled in all areas. The explanation was not due to a lack of technical understanding.

This is notable since Internet Explorer and Safari are the default browsers for Windows and Mac computers respectively, whereas Firefox and Chrome must be downloaded. This meant that Explorer and Safari users never bothered to look for a better browser and instead stuck with the one that came pre-installed. This is mirrored in their work as they chose to follow the script for phone conversations rather than create new ways to serve their consumers. They lacked initiative, which caused them to be dissatisfied at work and eventually resign.

It is only possible to succeed in life when we keep our minds open to all possibilities. There will always be one challenge or the other, no matter what you do. How you act in the face of a challenge determines where you'll go in life. Instead of complaining or giving up, learn from your surroundings wherever you go and find solutions, not problems. This is your way to move ahead in life.

Find solutions,

not problems.

Chapter 34

Luck Surface Area

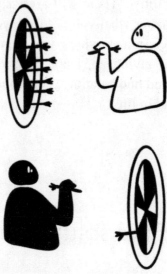

Much of what we call "luck" is the macro result of 1,000s of micro-actions.

Your habits put you in a position where luck is more likely to strike.

If you want to create more luck, increase your luck surface area.

Open up the aperture to let more luck in.

Luck is about the number of chances you take. The more chances you take, the luckier you get.

Over the span of two decades, William Shakespeare wrote thirty-seven plays and a hundred and fifty-four sonnets, even though he is remembered for only a few of them. He wrote *Othello*, *Macbeth* and *King Lear*, in the same years that he also wrote *Timon of Athens* and *All's Well That Ends Well*, which were considered among the worst of his plays. While he was developing perfect characters for the former three, he was also writing unpolished and incomplete prose for the latter two.

And there is no way to know how many ideas took birth in his brain but never got formed; how many ideas he started pursuing but abandoned midway; how many ideas he actually finished and then scrapped.

This pattern is easily visible in every field. We remember the five-year period of Thomas Elva Edison's life (between the ages of thirty and thirty-five), notable for his inventions like the light bulb, the photograph and the carbon telephone. But in the same period, he filed for more than a hundred patents for different things like a creepy talking doll, stencil pens, a way of using magnets to mine iron ore, and a fruit preservations technique. In his lifetime, he would go on to file for 1093 patents, out of which only a few would leave a mark on the sands of time.

Even Mozart, in spite of all his innate gifts, unmatched passion for music and his father's dedicated tutelage, needed to get twenty-four amateur symphonies before he composed his first respectable work, the twenty fifth one. In his short lifetime of only thirty-five years, he composed six hundred symphonies. Before he could write Così fan tutte, Mozart had practiced his scales. Similarly, Beethoven would go on to produce six hundred and fifty pieces of work, while Bach wrote over a thousand.

> *The correlation is easy to see.*
> *One has to kiss a lot of frogs*
> *before you find a prince.*

What are the elements that make a business successful? When chatting with and studying people we like, we are often reminded that success is a squiggly line, not a straight road. A person rarely achieves their goals only through the force of hard work.

In Alex Banayan's book *The Third Door*, the author spent his millennial life crisis on an astonishing 7-year search interviewing the world's most famous people on how they 'made it,' including Tim Ferriss, Bill Gates, Larry King, and others. He coined a brilliant analogy:

Success is like trying to enter an exclusive nightclub.

There is the front door for the 99% of people waiting in line, doing what everyone else is, and hoping to eventually get in.

There is the VIP door for the 1% in the privileged and connected who can effortlessly slip through.

What they don't tell you is that there is always a third door. This is through a back alley kitchen or a cracked window that will take resourcefulness to discover and guts to pound on.

Lesson:

There are always exceptions.

What if you were informed that you might improve your chances of becoming lucky? This, according to entrepreneur Jason Roberts, is entirely feasible. He coined the term 'Luck Surface Area' which allows you to have direct control over the quantity of serendipity in your life.

The quantity of activity you take around your passion, together with the number of individuals you convey your desire to, is known as Luck Surface Area.

The more you put your heart and soul into anything, the more you become an expert at it. The more people you tell about your passion, the more likely it is that good fortune will come your way. Some of the individuals you tell will gain value from your expertise in unexpected ways, which magnifies you even more.

This basic theory demonstrates that we keep the stabilisers on our metaphorical bicycles because of a lack of communication. To become 'luckier', we must convey our passions with vigour to those with whom we come into contact.

People are drawn to optimistic people who have enthusiasm and knowledge because their energy is contagious. Who knows what chances will present themselves out of sheer erendipity once we have dedicated time and efforts to our passions and explain our knowledge clearly.

Start Doing, Amplify With Telling

In his original post outlining this simple and powerful idea, entrepreneur and coder Jason Roberts explained that taking action towards your passion will develop expertise in that area.

When people become aware of your expertise, some percentage of them will take action to capture that value, but quite often it will be in a way you would never have predicted.

Roberts also pointed to the infectious nature of passion, and that taking action and sharing your passion will tend to attract others towards it, again amplified by the number of people who know about it.

Experiment And Take Risks

Tina Seelig, Stanford professor and the creator of *Framestorming*, has been studying entrepreneurs and luck for some time. Her reframing of how to view luck aligns well with this model. Seelig explains:

Luck is rarely a lightning strike, isolated and dramatic. It's much more like the wind, blowing constantly. Sometimes it's calm, and sometimes it blows in gusts. And sometimes it comes from directions that you didn't even imagine.

To 'catch luck' better, Seelig encourages you to consistently take small risks that push your comfort zone. In doing this, explore the types of risks you're willing to take, and identify where you might challenge yourself. For example, you might explore financial risk, investing money in something;

intellectual risk, playing with a new idea and challenging your assumptions; or social risk, talking to someone new.

Richard Wiseman, the author of the *Luck Factor*, agreed. His extensive research pointed to lucky people being the ones who were willing to continuously experiment and try new things.

Understanding The Luck Surface Area Better

Upworthy is an internet-based company that curates viral material. Coming up with headlines for the videos that motivate people to spread the content is a key part of their success.

The initial title they tried for a film of a guy talking about his lesbian parents was 'Zach Wahls speaks about family.' They modified it to 'Two lesbians raised a baby and this is what they got' when it didn't sell well. The latter exhibited a seventeen-fold increase in traction.

Upworthy had to submit a video of two monkeys receiving cucumber or grapes as a treat and reacting to it in another circumstance. 'Remember Planet of the Apes? You're closer to the truth than you realise' was the first title. '2 Monkeys Were Paid Unequally; See What Happens Next' was the second one. Which do you believe performed a better job?

The second headline performed five hundred and nine times better than the first. One criterion that Upworthy adheres to scrupulously is to generate at least twenty-five headlines before settling on one. They both believe that original concepts are the most common. They get their best ones once they've gotten out of the way.

'When you're desperate,' the Upworthy team writes, 'you start thinking outside the box. #24 is going to be a dud. Then #25 will be a gift from the gods of headlines, and you'll be a legend.'

Whatever field you study, you'll find that creative geniuses aren't necessarily those that come up with better ideas; they're no better than their counterparts in their fields. Instead, they are constantly coming up with new ideas.

> *They recognise that the chances of coming up with an excellent concept are proportional to the total number of ideas one can generate.*

It must be clear to you now that good things don't happen to lucky people; they make good things happen to themselves. Sitting around waiting for an opportunity will not land you that opportunity. Also, discrediting someone's success by saying 'they just got lucky' is also unfair to the person as you are discrediting their effort at creating the right conditions for luck to strike. Your luck awaits you, give it the chance to

Chapter 35

All Things Compounding

It's often said that compounding is a wonder.

But it doesn't just apply to money

Relationships, habits and progress also follow
compounding pattern

Have you ever wondered why Steven Spielberg and David Koepp have so many movies together? Steven Spielberg is one of the most influential and popular movie directors of all time, but perhaps it would be unfair to expect a man to excel both at directing and writing, which is why Spielberg leaves the latter responsibility to other people. David Koepp's prowess as a screenwriter is a big deal in itself, proved by the films he has written like *Jurassic Park* and its sequel, *Mission: Impossible* and *Spider-Man*.

But what makes both of them so special that they prefer working together? It's something that we call compounding of relationships, which is when you associate yourself with someone for a long time, you get comfortable around them and prefer working with them. This, in turn, acts similarly to the way money compounds when left for a long period of time. Relationships, too, appreciate with time.

> *The better you know your partner, the easier it is to work with them.*

When you work with someone you know, you can work without contracts and you are less likely to have a deviation of vision. You are aware of their idiosyncrasies and they are therefore less likely to derail the project. You will be more comfortable in receiving and giving critical feedback. The work ethic of all parties is familiar and one can plan accordingly.

> *Working on one sub-skill at a time provides a compounding effect that increases the overall skill.*

A skill can be broken down into several incremental steps or sub-skills. For instance, I've been playing basketball for over three decades. Although my fitness level has gotten worse over the last decade, I have continued to improve my skill set. I spent my adolescent years playing as much as possible without concentrating on any particular aspect of the play; and as a result, I did not improve.

However, when I was in my twenties, I learned to dribble and finish lay-ups with my weak hand. I learned to keep my head up when dribbling in my early thirties which increased my court awareness and allowed me to make better passes. I've spent the last ten years improving my shooting and rebounding. I've spent roughly ten to fifteen minutes every week on skill development for the past twenty years. While it may seem like a small period of time, these small changes have added up over the years to produce a significant difference in my game.

Relationships are likewise subject to the compounding effect. Relationship patterns accumulate over time and have far-reaching consequences. Relationship habits, on the other hand, are more subjective and less binary than financial investments. While your financial account can instantly tell you how well you're doing in the markets, assessing the strength of your relationships is more difficult. This means that our interpersonal patterns might amplify for the better or for the worse.

The compounding effect is often obscured since our wicked habits work against the righteous ones because each person is a mixed bag of behaviours. Our bad tendencies can easily outweigh our positive ones at any particular time.

Marriage is an example of relational habit compounding.

> *A good marriage is the result of the accumulation of healthy relationship habits, whereas a bad marriage is the result of the accumulation of unhealthy ones.*

Dr. John Gottman, a psychologist and clinician wrote on the habit of positive sentiment override. It is responding to a spouse with humour, encouragement, and/or re-direction to transform an unpleasant dialogue into a positive one. In this way, rather than choosing distance, a partner can de-escalate disagreement and make a play for emotional connection. This behaviour is also fuelled by your love and appreciation for your partner.

In my marriage with my wife, I've seen how good sentiment override has reversed unfavourable tendencies. I can make a joke, support her character, or change the subject instead of responding with contempt, anger, or irritability. I remember how tough this was at first, especially when it had little effect on the conversation's outcome, and it was emotionally draining to change my mood. Despite this, it has made our connection so much sweeter over time.

A relationship habit exercised in one moment rarely has an immediate effect, but it will certainly reap dividends in time—and that's the point. The success of relationship habit compounding should never be evaluated based on the short-term but rather over an extended period of time (meaning years or even decades), as momentum builds and the incremental effect accumulates.

* * *

The compounding effect is as relevant to your individual habits as it is to your relationships. When you practice a behavioural change for a few weeks, it turns into a habit. When you practice good habits for a few months or years, they yield a more productive and fulfilling life. While breaking a habit or building a new one may be difficult initially, it is only by facing these difficulties that you can change yourself for the better.

Sustained positive changes don't come in a day and never come easy. It takes a strong will to recognise and work on your habits. But once you break a bad habit or build a good one, you will not only have changed a habit but also increased your self-confidence.

Here's how you can compound on a relationship in order to grow better.

1. Maintain your identity

New relationships are incredibly thrilling and it's easy to get caught up in the excitement of discovering shared interests and ideas; but it's critical to maintain your individuality.

2. Create your own goals

Setting personal goals is a terrific approach to retain your sense of self—be it work-related goals or goals relating to exercise, dieting, or artistic pursuits. Devoting mental energy to goals focused on your self-improvement—and separate from your relationship—helps carve out much-needed personal space.

3. Compromise

Maintaining your identity and setting objectives isn't about putting yourself first over your spouse, so keep an open mind when it comes to the future of your relationship so that you and your partner may make mutually beneficial decisions as a team.

4. Understand your communication styles

Understanding your personal communication style as well as your partner's communication style can help you navigate misunderstandings and conflicts as partners in any field with more empathy and ease.

5. Embrace Tell Culture

While everyone has a preferred style of communication, articulating your needs clearly creates an authentic dialogue that will help you and your partner support each other.

6. Learn how to listen

Learning how to be a good listener is a huge asset to any long-term relationship. Being a good listener isn't limited to just active listening skills; it also involves understanding what your role should be in the conversation.

7. Check-in

It can be helpful to schedule relationship check-ins at regular intervals because they create a safe space for open communication to address certain negative feelings before they fester and cause a conflict. They can also be a time to praise your partner for things that are improving your relationship.

8. Respect

Respect is a key aspect of any kind of long-term relationship. You must respect your partner as an individual and as an equal in your relationship. It is also important to respect yourself in a relationship and not accept anything below your standard.

Having a few long-term connections throughout your life is critical. Once you've found at least one such relationship, you'll want to focus on compounding it. Remember that like money, everything else also takes time to multiply.

Patience is key.

The End

About the Author

Liam Finnian is a life coach who also works as an innovation consultant. He has trained more than five hundred individuals to transform their personal and work habits. He has also helped various business organizations solve problems in creative ways.

Through his interest and deep research on psychology, he has come up with solutions and mental models to live a more rational and well-thought-out life. His study has helped him develop a clear understanding of human behavior and motivation, which he uses to motivate his audience.

He lives in Illinois with his wife and two children. *Ideas To Grow Your Mind* is his first book. You can reach out to him at LiamFinnianBooks@gmail.com